The Reckoning Heart

Other Titles From New Falcon Publications

Cosmic Trigger: Final Secret of the Illuminati
Prometheus Rising
    By Robert Anton Wilson
Undoing Yourself With Energized Meditation
    By Christopher S. Hyatt, Ph.D.
Eight Lectures on Yoga
    By Aleister Crowley
Info-Psychology
The Game of Life
    By Timothy Leary, Ph.D.
Condensed Chaos: An Introduction to Chaos Magick
    By Phil Hine
The Challenge of the New Millennium
    By Jerral Hicks, Ed.D.
The Complete Golden Dawn System of Magic
    By Israel Regardie
Buddhism and Jungian Psychology
    By J. Marvin Spiegelman, Ph.D.
Astrology & Consciousness
    By Rio Olesky
The Eyes of the Sun: Astrology in Light of Psychology
    By Peter Malsin
Metaskills: The Spiritual Art of Therapy
    By Amy Mindell, Ph.D.
Changing Ourselves, Changing the World
    By Gary Reiss, LCSW
Soul Magic: Understanding Your Journey
    By Katherine Torres, Ph.D.
A Mother Looks At the Gay Child
    By Jesse Davis
Virus: The Alien Strain
    By David Jay Brown
Phenomenal Women: That's US!
    By Dr. Madeleine Singer

And to get your free catalog of *all* of our titles, write to:
New Falcon Publications (Catalog Dept.)
1739 East Broadway Road #1-277
Tempe, Arizona 85282 U.S.A
And visit our website at **http://www.newfalcon.com**

The Reckoning Heart
An Anthropologist Looks at Her Worlds

by
Manisha Roy, Ph.D.
(Author of BENGALI WOMEN)

NEW FALCON PUBLICATIONS
TEMPE, ARIZONA, U.S.A.

Copyright © 2001 by Manisha Roy

All rights reserved. No part of this book, in part or in whole, may be reproduced, transmitted, or utilized, in any form or by any means, electronic or mechanical, including photocopying, recording, or by any information storage and retrieval system, without permission in writing from the publisher, except for brief quotations in critical articles, books and reviews.

International Standard Book Number: 1-56184-149-8
Library of Congress Catalog Card Number: 00-104167

First Edition 2001

Cover by Amanda Fisher
Illustrated by Steven Solomon

The paper used in this publication meets the minimum requirements of the American National Standard for Permanence of Paper for Printed Library Materials Z39.48-1984

Address all inquiries to:
NEW FALCON PUBLICATIONS
1739 East Broadway Road #1-277
Tempe, AZ 85282 U.S.A.
(or)
320 East Charleston Blvd. • # 204-286
Las Vegas, NV 89104 U.S.A.

website: http://www.newfalcon.com
email: info@newfalcon.com

DEDICATION

In fond memory
of my father, Benoy Kumar Roy,
and of my teacher, the geographer and anthropologist
Nirmal Kumar Bose

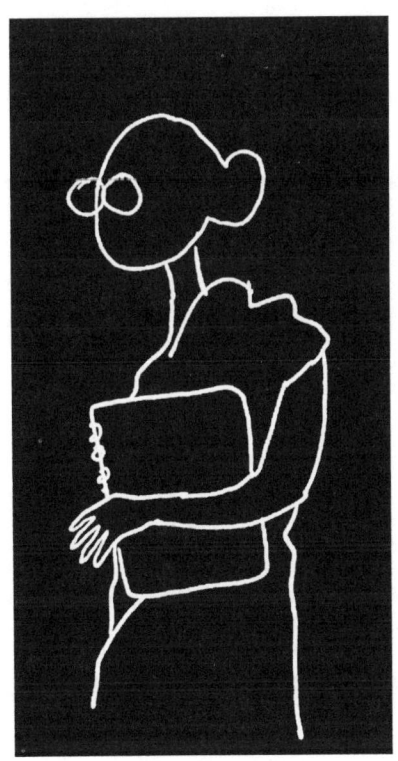

ACKNOWLEDGEMENTS

The pieces in this book were written at various points between 1966 and 1985 as entries in my journal, at the time of—or shortly after—the events that they describe. The first section, most of the second, and part of the third describe events that occurred during anthropological fieldwork. When I was in India, this followed the cycle of the seasons: of necessity, I would go to the field in winter and return before the monsoons, six months later. The fourth section is new ground. All the pieces in this book (with the exception of the opening one) were entered in my journal as stories, reporting actual events. This is because I experience the world around me in the form of stories. And now I can enjoy giving them back to the world. To me, this is anthropology—of a kind that transcends the traditional academic expectations. This book can also be read as an autobiography, not only of an anthropologist, but also of an analytical psychologist, which is what I am today.

I wish to acknowledge my gratitude to several people. First of all to my husband Carl F. von Essen who has been constant in his love and support throughout and who also helped in the preparation of the maps, I am eternally grateful. I thank Steven Solomon for his perseverance and talent in adorning this volume with the illustrations and maps. Jeffrey Haste helped by being an understanding friend in difficult times. My friend, poet and writer Georgiana Peacher's moral support and hospitality were invaluable. She, Paola Biola, Pat Carr, J. Marvin Spiegelman, Melford E. Spiro, and Susan Tiberghien all read the manuscript and gave constructive criticisms. I thank them all. And I thank all the people in these stories—who, in many ways, have changed my life. Their names, and in some cases the places they lived, have been changed in this book, for reasons of privacy.

TABLE OF CONTENTS

Until The Monsoons 11

Among The Hill-Tribes

Mother Lyndoh 23
An Invitation 31
Political Man 39
A Schoolteacher's Daughter 47

People Of The Plains

At Sunset 57
The Beggarwoman of Calcutta 65
Fertile Sand 73
A Marigold 79
Hospitable Strangers 89
On the Way to Pune 99

The West Coast Crowd

Welcome to California 109
Liberated Linda 123
The Uninvited Informant 137

In The Land Of The Swiss

Gossip and Legend 149
Swiss Encounters 159
The Neighborly Frau Buechli 169
Herr Professor's Birthday 177

Epilogue 185

About the Author 187

Until The Monsoons

One evening in the spring of 1966, in my very first weeks of fieldwork as an anthropologist, I went to my tent to write my daily report *and could not recall what observations I had made that day.* I sat there and struggled to make sense of the vague images and nameless fragments of thought that flickered across my consciousness only to fade away irretrievably. It was as if I had amnesia.

With one strange exception, I could not remember any of the interviews I had conducted, and this despite the presence of pages of shorthand notes I had made every time. I could, however, remember all the other events of the day, and the conversations, word for word, which were not "relevant" to my research. I was frightened. Only the interview with an angry political activist could I reproduce with any satisfaction. In that encounter I had been affected by the strength of the informant's emotions about the plight of his people. I had become less objective.

I was working in India among the Khasis, a hill-tribe of central Assam.[1] From the data I was gathering, I would make an analysis of the factors contributing to the conflict between the Khasis and the immigrant Nepalese. For two or three decades, the Nepalese had been moving into the sparsely-populated hills of Assam, some five hundred miles southeast of Nepal. They had come, initially, in search of pastures for their cattle. But then, through clever bureaucratic maneuvers, they began to "take over" the Khasiland. The natives were only lately catching on to this. As they did, the tension and animosity grew and accelerated. And now, because of my "amnesia," it looked as if my good, hard work would prove useless to understanding this conflict.

---

[1] This area became the Indian state of Meghalaya in 1972.

In effect, what I could easily recall of that otherwise impenetrable day were the people themselves: how they felt about their world, about their lives. So, to deal with the anxiety mounting inside me, I began to make notes on this aspect of things, on the impressions I received of people, rather than on the facts I was collecting about their institutions. This approach helped. The crisis ebbed. By morning, my memory had returned.

Thus developed another set of field-notes that soon covered many pages, becoming as essential to my survival as to the success of my work.

This book was born from these pages in my field-notes. It was only natural for me, when I transcribed the notes into my journal, to put them in the form of stories. Several of the pieces collected here were written between 1966 and 1971, when I was actively engaged in anthropology. Others were written in my travels to one country or another, when my life had taken a surprising new turn.

Many of the journeys I have made around the world and throughout my life, I now know, were not simply explorations of countries and cultures, but also of my own inner landscape. One aspect of this exploration—both external and internal, I believe—is that of my being a stranger or outsider. For the first fifteen years of my life, I lived in an area culturally and linguistically different from that in which my family originated.[2] Since the age of twenty-one, I have been living in what are to me, foreign countries. Throughout my life I have been aware of being a marginal person. And yet, my journeys may have helped me, as well—to struggle with and to appreciate this position, and to benefit from it.

The geographical pattern of my travels went westward from Digboi, my birthplace, near the Burmese border of Assam, in the easternmost corner of India. At fifteen I left for Calcutta, some nine hundred miles west, to attend college. Six years later I traveled another ten thousand miles west, to North America, for graduate school. The first story in this book was written when, as a student of anthropology, I had returned east again; in fact, back to Assam. Since then I have traveled east and west, north and

---

[2] My family are Bengali Hindus.

south, many times, as if to discover myself from as many directions as possible.

Another aspect of this exploration is the incongruity between the explicit purpose of my travels and what actually happened. Whether my travels were for fieldwork, or to lecture or teach, or simply for tourism, I would encounter obstacles in my psyche that made me aware of something more profound. Certain of these experiences changed my view of life, others awakened in me an otherwise dormant sense of values that had been overshadowed by a newer and more fashionable one.

Discoveries of human character—the eccentric, the normal, with virtues and vices, the kindness, sacrifice, cruelty, and humor—all came when least expected. These were, by turns, delightful, adventurous, irritating, and problematic. I learned more about the contradictory beauty of human nature than I could imagine. Many of these discoveries came during what was deemed abortive research: by-products, as it were, of otherwise failed situations.

After the fateful bout of amnesia in the field, it was clear that I could conduct my scientific research only if I paid attention, as well, to those observations I was trained to circumvent by calling them "soft data" or "irrelevant information." Despite my attraction to them, I knew no way to use those observations in the proposed anthropological research.

I was not alone in this conundrum. Many anthropologists before and after me have had similar experiences.[3] For myself, the more I saw the conflict yet proceeded to gather two kinds of information, the more I realized that eventually I must bring the two together. The sacrifice of one or the other could create in me a serious emotional problem. At the time I was working in the field, the marriage of the two seemed impossible. I ended up writing a "scientific" monograph and putting the soft data away in a file.

I had an intuition that the marriage would have to take place within myself. I would have to bring the two sides of myself

---

[3] See Collin M. Turnbull, *The Forest People,* 1961, and *The Mountain People,* 1972; Manda Cesara, *Reflections of a Woman Anthropologist: No Hiding Place,* 1982; and Mary Catherine Bateson, *Peripheral Visions: Learning Along the Way,* 1994.

together. It took another decade and a few more professional crises for that to happen.

The dilemma I had experienced in the field soon took on other forms. In my effort to attend to the personal element, I had not recognized that human nature can be not only unpredictable and beautiful, but also disturbing and destructive. Only later did I understand that the confusion I faced with other cultures actually mirrored the confusion within myself. The demands of outer adjustment helped me to bring emotions into the process, exposing my own paradoxical self. The professional conflicts and personal problems could no longer be separate. But I am getting too far ahead of myself. Let me go back....

When I was a student of cultural anthropology, I was concerned about certain questions. What exactly is the tenuous connection between an individual and the culture? When does a cultural tradition cease to offer security to its members and instead becomes so confining that one must protest or rebel to survive as an individual? Who are "the deviants," the exceptions? What is their function in a society? These questions not only attracted me to the more humane information in the field, but also led me, eventually, to the depth of my own psyche. This is because these questions lay at the bottom of my own identity and of my relationship to my own and other cultures.

Six years of theory, of courses fraught with jargon and complex methodologies of research, were tolerable only because of the hope of an escape to the field. All anthropologists wait for the day when they can at last make that pilgrimage. When these sophisticated courses took me farther and farther away from the human beings I hoped to understand better, I anxiously looked forward to getting an answer in the field, where I would encounter the subject matter in flesh and blood.

By then I knew that my life had a plan that was, as yet, concealed from me. It was like a thread, weaving a pattern I was not yet wise enough to see. How else could I explain several so-called coincidences? For example: When I first came to America, it was to a university that had accepted me as a student by mistake—it had no graduate degrees in my field, which was then Geography. I was, instead, invited to enter the department of Anthropology. I had no background in the subject, but Nirmal

Kumar Bose, my Geography professor at Calcutta University, happened as well to be a highly-recognized anthropologist. This coincidence encouraged me to make the switch. But in a way, I had been a secret anthropologist for a long time....

When I was a girl in the little oil-town of Digboi in Assam, I occasionally saw tribal people who had come down from the frontier—from the foothills of the Himalayas. They appeared mysterious and strange, coming as they did from the distant mountains which looked from my windows like dark blue clouds. Long sacks of bark-cloth hung from their bare shoulders. They wore very little clothing.

When we, the children of Digboi, refused to drink our cod-liver oil every morning, our mothers told us that these half-naked strangers would grab us and put us into their sacks and we would never return. They were supposed to be head-hunters. Although mildly afraid, I did not quite believe these threats. I had already observed that the sacks contained rather harmless though fascinating items such as resin, honey, exotic bird feathers, animal skins, and occasional pieces of ivory. The tribal people used these items to barter for tobacco, sugar, tea, and so forth.

My curiosity about strangers and their lives began then, and so did my life-long habit of recording my observations: I have kept a journal since that time. I had begun my anthropological fieldwork long before I was trained to do so formally.

I did not think of this childhood experience while at the university trying to learn how anthropologists before me had done their research. Instead, I studied how to construct a logically consistent hypothesis to be tested in the field, as well as to discard data that could not prove or disprove such a hypothesis. My goal was to write a dissertation that would be accepted by an academic committee, if not by anyone else. Nonetheless, my decision to return to India for my first fieldwork was due more to homesickness than to anything of a professional nature.

When I returned to Calcutta from America, I had the good fortune to find a research position at the Anthropological Survey of India, an agency of the central government. I would have ample opportunity for all the fieldwork I wanted. To my delight, I was posted to Shillong, a charming city at over 6,000 feet above sea level, in the same state where I was born. To study the

Khasi tribe was then the natural choice; Shillong was in the middle of the Khasiland, a beautiful area of hills, plateaus, and valleys. The Khasis are a Sino-Burmese tribe, one of the few remaining matrilineal societies in the world. They lived within a hundred miles of either side of the sixty-mile paved road—the only link at the time—between Shillong and Gauhati, the two largest cities in the state.

I spent six months in Shillong while all the necessary preparations were made. I would sit in my little office, warming my feet over a charcoal brasier beneath the desk, looking out at the pine forests on the hillsides. I felt the same thrill of anticipation I had felt many times before. At last I would be a bona fide anthropologist, about to face "my people" in the remote country outside civilization (even though the distance between Shillong and the interior villages I was about to visit was not more than fifty miles).

Every night before falling asleep I would imagine different scenarios for my days with the people. These would range from routine interviews to a dangerous riot, or an earthquake, which would pose a situation unprecedented in the history of anthropological fieldwork. Sometimes I would make long lists of essentials to take with me. I must not forget typing paper in three colors, I noted, so that I can make three separate copies of my field-notes in case two of them get lost. I had remembered an anecdote about the British anthropologist Radcliffe-Brown, who had once lost all his notes in a New Guinea flood. After that, he had always advised his students to make three different copies of all field-notes—in three colors.

I remembered what Bronislaw Malinowski, the father of anthropological fieldwork, said in his diaries. At times he hated the people with whom he lived, and the loneliness was unbearable. But even these apprehensions could not dampen my enthusiasm.

I could not wait to brave those unpaved, unmarked roads that would take me to the remote world awaiting my exploration. Exotic places whose names I had not yet learned to pronounce—Umkynsir, Umsaw, Nongpoh, Nongladew—would not just be dots on the map but real places I would visit and in which I would set up my camp. I could see myself struggling to keep awake while typing my notes in the meager light of a kerosene lamp in my tent, after a long day's work. The monotonous sound of the tropical crickets cutting into the dark evening outside, and the faint chatter of the cook and the driver in the next tent, would make the scene complete.

Yes, it would be lonely with a driver and a cook who not only did not "speak my language," but definitely did not share my romantic notions about the work. Somehow the anticipation of such loneliness made the prospect of adventure even more tantalizing. With such musings I would fall asleep at last.

Two days before I was to start, Professor Bose, who had himself conducted fieldwork in the area, flew in from Calcutta to see me off. He succeeded in bringing me back to earth with advice on many practical questions. I must be very careful with the drinking water. It is always safe to drink tea. He gave me tips on how to abstain from local food without insulting the host. I must avoid driving after dark and must not neglect to transcribe my notes every evening, regardless of how tired I might be. And, of course, I must finish the fieldwork before June, when the monsoons[4] were expected.

We sat over a sheaf of maps which I had marked with red, blue, and green pencils many times already. He suggested some camp-sites and warned me against the road maps that were made by the Public Works Department long before the roads were even built—or might ever be. (Later, a P.W.D. surveyor in one of the interior villages confessed to me that he was advised to prepare such maps.)

Next day, Professor Bose introduced me to Reverend Lyndoh, a Khasi whom he had met on one of his field-trips in the area. The Reverend, all of five feet in his white robe and sandals, smiled broadly, which left four deep furrows on either side of his tiny mouth and eyes. As I watched his face with fascination, he stretched out his plump hand to take mine in a firm grip, giving me a sense of security I did not expect.

"No problem, no problem," he said to the professor in perfect English. "She will be most welcome in my home, where my mother will look after her." He smiled at me again. We all smiled and nodded while Reverend Lyndoh bowed in the oriental manner and shook hands again to say goodbye.

---

[4] This is the season of heavy torrential rains of the tropics, arriving in June and ending in September.

When the Reverend had left, the professor told me how dedicated a pastor he was to his villagers of the Khasi tribe. Staying with his mother would not only be good protection, but also good strategy. I thanked the professor for all the help and advice.

"Yes," I said. "Between the two fathers, I surely am well taken care of, body and soul."

"It's the Reverend's mother who will take care of your body, if not your soul," he responded, with a twinkle of his eye. "And mind you, she does not speak a word of English. And as for your soul, I suggest a couple of good novels and a short-wave radio." That night I barely slept.

In the morning, as I climbed into the loaded jeep next to the driver, I was handed a bottle of aspirin and an old paperback copy of Joseph Conrad's *The Heart of Darkness*.

"The professor left these for you early this morning, before leaving for the airport," said the driver.

Suddenly I was sad that I had not properly said goodbye to such a caring father, who had come all the way from Calcutta to see me off.

The jeep took its way down the town roads, and the morning sun hit my eyes. I forgot the sadness for the moment.

"This is it," I told myself. *"At last!"*

Among The Hill-Tribes

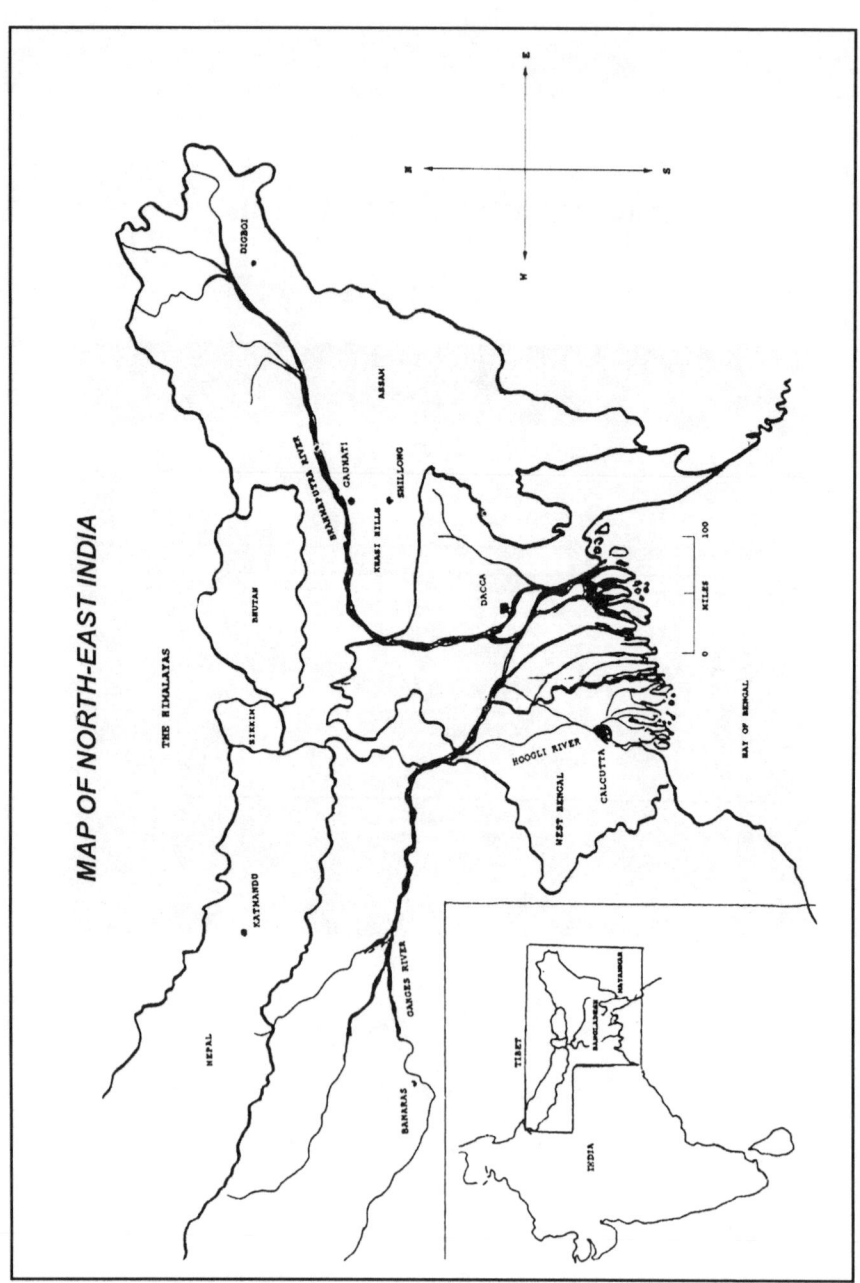

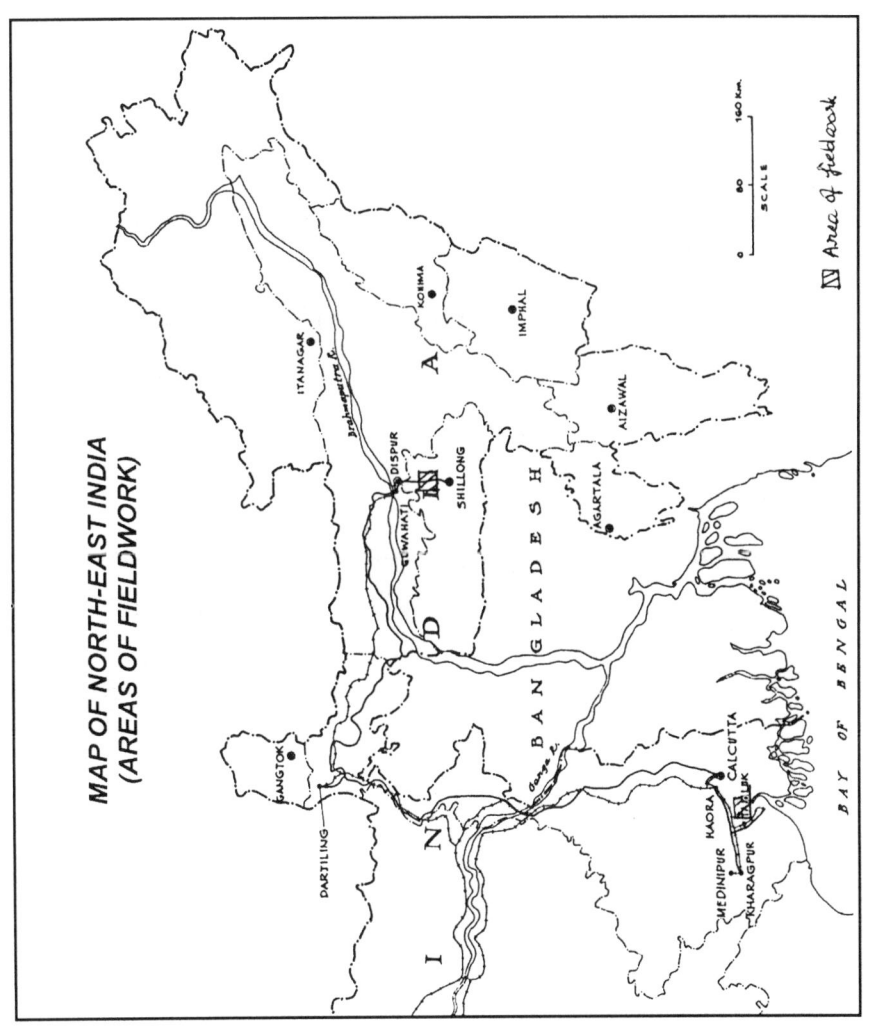

Mother Lyndoh

The jeep went along the paved road, leaving behind the city of Shillong. The words, "No problem, no problem," meant by Reverend Lyndoh to be reassuring, lingered in my mind like a tune that would not stop repeating itself. By the day's end, I thought, I will at least have a place to stay. It doesn't matter whether his mother speaks English or not.

Without warning, we left the asphalt and began slowly to make our way to the interior through a valley, on what looked like a dry riverbed. It was rocky, and I held tight to the dashboard so as not to fall in the laps of the driver or the guide, between whom I sat. The two of them seemed well-practiced in such rough travel.

Tom, the guide, a jaunty Khasi aged twenty or so, had been recruited by someone in my office as interpreter and assistant for the duration of my fieldwork. He claimed to know the territory like the palm of his hand. From the moment we picked him up at his cousin's house in downtown Shillong, he had not stopped talking. I wished now I had had the opportunity to interview him before he was offered the job.

"I know all about your line of work," he said, as if he were aware of my doubts about him. "I wanted to become an anthropologist myself. But that will have to wait for now. I need to go to America first." He leaned forward to hang half of his body out the side of the jeep and spit a jet of red betel[5] juice onto the roadside. Bahadoor, the driver, a Nepalese, sat ramrod stiff and paid no attention to Tom—or to me, though I kept bouncing and bounding against him.

"You see," said Tom, as he put a fresh quid of betel into his mouth, "I know a lot about America, not just about my own

---

[5] The betel nut is the seed of the areca palm. It is wrapped with other ingredients in a heart-shaped leaf and chewed.

country. I get *Reader's Digest* every month. I study everything in it carefully." He paused, as if to contemplate the breadth of his learning. "I am saving money, and with your help I will soon fulfill my dream of going to America." I turned my eyes on him at this, but he had not finished.

"The only problem is this habit of mine," he said, and leaned his body out of the jeep to spit again. "I don't understand why such a clever nation has not yet discovered the chewing of betel. If they would try once they will forget their chewing-gums forever. In fact, I may become the first person to introduce betel-chewing to that country. All I need is a government permit to export. What do you think of the idea?"

I thought only of changing the subject. "Tom, what made those odd furrows on the hillsides?" I asked. "And the hills look so bare. Why is that?"

"Oh, it's those Nepalese bastards," he said moodily. "They graze their cattle everywhere. Those furrows as you call them are ledges made by the hooves of the cattle, who have eaten up all the vegetation. They are ruining our beautiful hills." The driver showed no response to these remarks. "But what do you think about my idea of exporting betel?" Tom's anger was short-lived. I looked again at the hills.

"When I heard that you had studied in America," he went on, "I immediately applied for this job. Otherwise, I have plenty to do. Everyone needs Tom to mediate among the headmen, the politicians, the government officials. You see, not many Khasis speak Nepalese, Hindi, *and* English. I am wanted everywhere." He leaned out to spit again. I took the opportunity to say a few words of my own.

"Look, Tom. You are being paid for this job. I want you to understand that there is no other kind of exchange involved. I would be happy to help you after I finish my work here. Right now, let's concentrate on the task at hand." I should have stopped there. "Besides, going to America is not so simple. You need certain qualifications."

"That's not a difficulty. I have it all written up and typed out for you. It's all here," he assured me, and pointed to his bags in the back seat, piled next to the cook, who sat silently the whole ride.

"Memsahib," said Bahadoor, coming to my rescue, "do you wish to stop for lunch?" The jeep slowed and I looked out at a cluster of roadside huts: tea shops and small grocers. One storefront, with a few plastic chairs and bare wooden tables set up outdoors, appeared to be the only restaurant, if one could call it that. The place was not at all inviting, but the aroma of spices had drifted to us and I hesitated.

"No, no. This place is too dirty," said Tom. "Five miles up the road is a place where we can get fresh-cooked rice and chicken curry and some local fruit. Let's move on."

"That sounds good to me," I said. The idea of fresh fruit had convinced me, rather than any desire to agree with Tom.

The place up the road turned out to be one that served rice beer. I saw Tom filling an empty bottle. We ate hurriedly and I had no time to explore. When we started the ride again, Tom seemed quieter. Perhaps it was the rice beer in the middle of the day. I was pleased to have this respite and could now pay more attention to my surroundings.

The jeep scuttled along a dirt road that ran upon the hillsides, considerably higher than the valleys—above which we were now passing. The sun was still strong, though it was almost four in the afternoon. People could be seen in the distance. They looked like specks, moving up or down the hills with tall, tapered baskets on their backs. They were mostly women and the baskets were almost as tall as they themselves. They walked uphill with a stoop. The baskets held cloth bundles of vegetables or grain. One woman was close enough for us to see, in her basket, a dozing baby, rocking rhythmically with the mother's steps.

The shops and food-stalls we encountered were run mostly by women, although many of their customers were men. I mentioned this to Bahadoor, the driver.

"Memsahib, Khasi women are very hard-working and independent. They have no time for the likes of him," he said, and gestured toward Tom, who was now asleep. "I used to know some Khasi women in Shillong..." He stopped. I waited, and did not pry. He did not go on. I was glad to have had even this small chance to talk with Bahadoor, a man of few words. I felt I would be secure trusting him, though I knew the political situation in the Khasiland was not very favorable to him. I hoped that the Khasi-Nepalese conflict would not be reflected inside our little group. It was strange that these two people, Tom and Bahadoor, on whom I would have to depend in the field, belonged to "enemy camps."

We took a turn and climbed a bit higher, where now the trees and vegetation grew more densely. We passed a slender waterfall, so close I could feel its cool spray. The sudden change of scenery reminded me of eastern Assam, where I had lived as a child. I remembered many jeep rides into the hills and jungles, where lush green trees and vines made everything cool and dark. These were picnic trips with my family and friends. We children loved to wander near the deep jungles, perhaps following the faint sound of a waterfall, half wishing to encounter a herd of wild elephants. The adults would be busy setting up temporary cook-fires. Those were wonderful Sundays of food, laughter, play—and adventure. I had felt quite at ease outside our civilized oil-town because I was with friends and protected by the adults. I closed my eyes under the warmth of my memories. I wished now I could share them with someone. Would Bahadoor understand?

One of the tires struck a rock and I was jolted out of my reverie. I opened my eyes to the magnificent glow of the western sky. Since we were heading almost due north, the whole sky to our left was rose, amber, and purple. Beside me, Tom was stretching his legs and yawning. Following my gaze, Bahadoor asked if I would like to stop for a few minutes to watch the sunset.

"No, no," put in Tom, adamantly. "We must not waste time now. It will be hard to find our way in the village if we arrive after dark. We still have to cover several miles." Knowing how suddenly the night falls in these lands, I was forced to agree with him again.

The jeep went on, and we watched the glorious sky softening its colors until it was dark enough that the shadows cast by the boulders on either side of the road began to melt away into the deeper darkness beyond them. A Khasi woman with a basket on her back stopped to watch our progress for a moment before walking away into a valley. She, too, melted away. Suddenly all was dark. Night had fallen. After another mile, we began to descend the high hills. Tom pointed out a few dim lights in the distance: a village. Our destination, *"Mawbri."*

I pronounced the name aloud and looked at the lights blinking through patches of fog and smoke in the valley below us. Three waves of dark blue hills surrounded the village. I was reminded of a movie I had once seen, in which a sixteenth-century Japanese village became slowly visible through the evening fog. It was a samurai movie and what happened in that dream-like place was not very beautiful or peaceful. I wondered if my future in this place would be equally disturbing. Right now, Mawbri in fog and smoke promised something new and mysterious.

After a few wrong turns, we found the little house of Reverend Lyndoh's mother. Bahadoor parked the jeep. I got out and followed Tom on foot along a narrow path cool from the evening dew. The houses, not more than huts, were spaced well apart from one another. The impression was that there were not many people in the village. But then, I could hardly see, it was so dark.

Tom went inside the house. I waited outside in the smoky, encircling fog. I shivered slightly in the damp air. I was alone, standing in the dark in a Khasi village whose people and language I did not know. Though only forty miles from a city where I was completely at home, I now felt abandoned and utterly lonely. "What on earth am I doing here?" I asked under my breath.

Tom appeared, with another figure, at the door of the house. He introduced Mother Lyndoh to me. She bowed, and murmured something in her language. I stood stiffly, not knowing how to greet this woman whose customs I did not know. I extended my hand to shake hers, but instead of taking it, she bowed again. Tom reminded me that she did not speak a word of English, but that she understood the situation, for he had explained everything to her. Reverend Lyndoh had written, of course, to make proper arrangements. I should not have any difficulties, I was told.

Now we were inside the house. In the flickering light of the charcoal fire that burned on a sheet of tin in the middle of the room, I noticed that Mother Lyndoh had the same small-featured face as her son, although her hair was grey and long, tied in a braid that dangled down her broad back. Her eyes, too, were lost in furrows when she smiled. Her teeth were black from chewing tobacco, a practice common among the older people in that part of the country.

Tom went to help Bahadoor and the cook to unload the jeep, while I looked around at this place that would be my home for the next three weeks. Mother Lyndoh watched me. She walked to one corner of the room and spread out a bamboo mat. She patted it, calling to me with a smile. I went to her and sat on the mat. She rose to poke the charcoal fire a bit and then took an aluminum kettle down from a hook that hung from the bamboo roof. She looked at me with a questioning smile. I nodded. She began to make tea.

Three cups hung from pegs on the bamboo wall. A cigarette can of dried tea, an old strainer, and a small pan of milk had been set out on the floor. I watched her. She was in her sixties or seventies. Yet her plump hands, with their small round fingers, and her braided hair and round head, made her look like a little girl. Her smooth yellow skin looked tight and firm in the glow of the charcoal fire. She put spoons of dried tea, sugar, and milk in a cup before pouring hot water from the kettle, which she held between her hands.

I got up to help. The kettle looked very heavy for her. She smiled and put the kettle down, took my hands in hers, and giggled—as if to tell me that my hands were no good for such work, that I could not possibly pick up a hot kettle of that size. I gave up and giggled back, agreeing with her, and sat down to drink my tea. She gestured to me to wait, then took a piece of ginger root from a basket and cut a sliver from it with a small paring knife, and smiled at me before dropping it in my teacup. She sniffed, pulling her flat little nose, to tell me that the ginger root would protect me from getting a cold. I laughed at the funny face she had made and nearly choked on the ginger tea. But for the first time since leaving Shillong, I relaxed. I felt comfortable, I enjoyed the warmth of the tea and the charcoal fire and the woman I had just met.

Bahadoor and Tom came with my things and put them in a corner of the room. She offered them some tea but they declined, and left, I supposed, to camp somewhere. Perhaps Tom knew of a place where they could drink something stronger than tea. I went to the door and called to Tom's disappearing figure to remind him to come by in the morning to take me to the headman[6]. I was not sure that he even heard me.

Mother Lyndoh placed a bamboo rod across the door. The day was fast ending. I felt the smoke around me, enveloping, bringing my world closer to hers. I finished the tea, and now my eyes were smarting from the smoke. She looked at me with small twinkling eyes as if to say, "Well, we must have a fire, otherwise you'd be cold, my dear. Better get used to the smoke." I smiled back to tell her that I'd be all right. She took our cups to a bucket of water to wash them. The water drained down through the bamboo floor to the ground below. She took me by the hand and led me to what appeared to be the toilet, a sort of unlit closet on one side of the hut, built over a pit in the ground below.

She spread two mats in the center of the room, near the fire, like two spokes of a wheel, and bent down over my bedroll. After struggling with the leather strap for a few minutes, she giggled, showing me her plump palms which were no good for such jobs. I undid the knot, feeling quite at home now. In my enthusiasm I offered her a blanket, but she declined. She pointed to the fire: it would keep her warm enough. We stretched out on our mats. My wristwatch read only quarter to eight, but the village was already quiet.

I lay in my bed breathing the charcoal smoke, wondering how huts might be built to release the smoke more effectively without letting in the cold air. Soon I felt terribly tired, and before I had time to mull over my first evening in the field, I was asleep. The last thing I remembered was the soft sporadic snoring coming from the other mat. I felt very safe.

I do remember a dream from that night. I was with my grandmother in her village, several hundred miles away in West Bengal. She was telling me a tale, as she used to do when I was a child. But her eyes looked very small and her teeth looked rather black. But my grandmother does not chew tobacco, I told myself in the dream.

— *1966* —

---

[6] Tribal leader.

An Invitation

It was a morning in March. I had the same schedule every day, from morning till sundown—or till I was exhausted. My journal entries, though dated numerically, were not kept according to which day of the week it happened to be, so I had no idea what day it was. Then, walking at the edge of the heavily-wooded village of Lerkhla, I heard a choir...singing in *Latin!*

I had been talking to Tom about my need to interview a Khasi political figure of some sort. I stopped in the middle of a sentence and stared into the trees in disbelief. I had heard it: the unmistakable sound of voices lifted in pure praise. A choir was singing a hymn, though in a rough and amateur fashion.

"Oh, there he goes again," said Tom. "Out to get more converts. It would be better if that priest were to put some business ideas before the people, rather than teach them to sing and pray." He made a move in another direction, away from the singing. I, however, did not move.

"But you never told me there was a church around here," I said. "Let's take a look." I set off toward the sound of the choir.

"I didn't think you were here to study Christianity," Tom called after me, in an effort to discourage my advance. "And there is no church. It's just a crazy priest who holds a service wherever he can. He makes a few people sing 'in praise of the Lord.' The people are so stupid that they would listen to anyone who is big and tall."

My curiosity grew the nearer we came to the singers themselves, whom we found in a small clearing in the trees. About twenty people, mostly women and children, were sitting on reed mats or little wooden stools and benches, facing a small table draped in white linen. A leather-bound book lay on the table and next to it stood a vase of fresh wild lilies. At the table stood a tall man in a worn white robe that looked as if it needed laundering, moving his arms gently back and forth, conducting the choir, a few teen-aged boys and girls. His back was toward us.

It was obvious that the tall man was the priest to whom Tom had referred. It was also obvious that he was a foreigner, quite a bit bigger and taller than the small-statured Khasis. I stood slightly behind the little congregation, listening to the singing, and I realized that it must be Sunday.

I felt that things were oddly out of joint; as if, for a moment, I were standing in a town-square in medieval Europe, listening to a group of humble celebrants, their voices, like their church spire, rising upward into the clouds....

The singing stopped and the people began to scatter. The priest picked up the Bible. A Khasi woman removed the linen cloth from the table and gave it to him, neatly folded. He in turn gave her the flowers, then emptied the vase of water and tucked it somewhere into the folds of his robe. Before Tom could stop me, I approached him.

I introduced myself, and added how pleasantly surprised I was to find him in the middle of nowhere trying to bring his God to a people who were so different from himself. He at first made no sign that he had heard my comment, but extended a long hand from his robe and took my hand, then made a broad grin that was partly obscured in his dark, reddish beard.

"I am Father Angelo," he said. "That's what everyone calls me. I also am very surprised—to see you, a woman from 'civilization.' You have courage. Anthropology, yes, it's very interesting. What exactly are you doing?" He stopped, looking slightly ill at ease, as if he had said too much.

From his name, accent, and style of speech, I was certain he came from Italy. Something about him and his words bore so simple a generosity that I was embarrassed about my previous comment. I wanted to make up somehow. I asked if he had time for lunch so that we could talk about things. After all, I thought to myself, he could give me information I could not get from the villagers—or from Tom, for that matter.

"The only restaurant in the area is my kitchen," said the priest, laughing heartily, "and I would be delighted to accept your invitation for a meal in my hut, if you like. But I cannot have lunch."

I smiled, grateful.

"I have several more services to perform," he said, "and I'm already late. Please tell me where you are staying. I shall come this evening to fetch you—or perhaps this young man could bring you to my house."

Tom was reluctant to help. "I know where you live," he said, grudgingly.

"Wonderful!" said the priest to me. "I shall see you at five. Do you eat meat?"

"*Yes,*" I exclaimed. He moved away in long strides before I could say anything else.

Tom was not pleased about this turn of events. Since the very beginning of his employment, Tom had been behaving more like a guardian than an assistant, and was always eager to guard me from the attention of others. This protection began to feel to me like uncalled-for restriction. I did not know how to tell him this without offending him, because I knew he meant well.

Tom's irritation was clear now. He told me that he did not think it was a good idea to have dinner with the priest. The village leaders might read other things into such a visit. With some difficulty, I kept myself from asking, "What other things?"

"I want to get some information from the priest about the rate and reasons of conversion of the villagers," I said. "He may also give me information about the local history and politics that others will not—or cannot. Besides, I would not mind the taste of different food for a change."

As soon as I said this I felt annoyed with myself for needing to convince Tom of my plans. I was his employer, not the other way around. Why did I need to explain anything to him? Was it because I knew that I was partly at his mercy when finding my way in this unknown land and culture? I had to admit that he did have contacts I needed. But this time I would use the contact that had just dropped from the blue—or, more appropriately, from heaven. I had to find a way to put Tom in his place without making an issue of everything. Six years in America had given me the sort of habits that accompany democratic ideals, evident here in my confusion over how to treat one's subordinates.

I felt a little better when it occurred to me that, perhaps, I was also witnessing something primordial, but quite normal, among the males of the species—such as competition or territoriality. Father Angelo not only spoke perfect English but was much bigger than Tom in size and charm. And, of course, Tom was not interested in anyone who was not American or connected to America in some way.

But Tom was persistent. He tried to dissuade me with some gossip about these priests, who meddle with the local politics by "brain-washing" the villagers, not only into their religion but also into political factions. Of course, I myself had read the news that lately hit the headlines of the national papers. One well-known Catholic priest who had been in the neighboring Mizoland was now in severe trouble with the central government because of such meddling.

"Would it be wise to associate with someone like him who is not really useful for our work?" said Tom.

"Tom, let me be the judge of that, please." With this I moved toward my tent and called the cook to serve lunch. I went to take a quick shower in the make-shift enclosure built for that purpose. Two buckets of water were kept in the roofless stall to be warmed by the sun, a practice common in winter in the villages of India. It was good to wash away the dust—and the discussion.

While I ate my bowl of rice and vegetables in my tent, I kept wondering if the priest's dinner promised a leg of lamb. After several weeks of meatless fare, such a fantasy made my mouth water. But how to keep Tom out of the evening's experience? He had as uncanny a capacity to act on my conscience as my high school headmistress had in my teens. I would become overly serious about work and always spoil the fun that might come of freedom and surprise.

I knew I had a job to do. I would have to finish my research before the onset of the rainy season. But I could not be a robot. Nowhere in his letters and conversations did Professor Bose ever say that I had to work all the time. Arguing with myself thus, I dozed off. I had a fleeting dream that I was in a small town in Italy and Father Angelo was showing me a medieval cathedral.

"Madam," called the cook from outside the tent. "The tea is ready." When I came out I saw Father Angelo standing with Bahadoor, conversing in Hindi. He turned to me with a glint in his grey eyes.

"I was not far from here and thought I might take you back with me, if you don't mind, although it's not yet five. This way you could release your young man for the evening. He must have other plans." He noticed my surprise. "Oh, someone in the village told me where your tents were pitched." His gaze moved across the camp-site. "Lovely," he said, as he walked around. I was delighted. Here was the opportunity I was hoping for. I looked around for Tom, but Bahadoor told me that he had gone to the village to get the newspaper.

"I would be most happy to tell Tom that you left for dinner early," said Bahadoor. "I will come later with the jeep to bring you back to the camp-site, if that is what you wish."

While I ran to get a sweater, Father Angelo told Bahadoor to come by around eight o'clock, and gave him directions to the house. For once, Tom had no part in these matters. I felt secure in my position.

Father Angelo and I walked single-file nearly three quarters of an hour, on the edge of hill terraces or on dirt paths, before we reached his village. We talked little. I kept my eyes on the path, noticing that his large canvas shoes looked rather worn and old.

I could see only the thatched roof when he pointed out his hut. It was encircled by Scotch pines. We wound along a grassy path to the door. A sliver of veranda lay in front of the hut, with a wooden bench and a couple of old rattan chairs to furnish it. Its mud floor was hard and clean. He crossed it and pushed open the unlocked door, then stepped aside.

"Welcome to my humble house, please."

He stooped when he followed me in, to avoid hitting his head on the door-frame. The room was lit by the last rays of sun. I could see shelves of books on two walls, and a narrow bed covered with a reed mat. Father Angelo went into the other room, the kitchen. He came back with an oil lamp—and asked if I wanted to sit outside or join him in the kitchen. I, of course, opted for the latter, and sat on a wooden stool in the kitchen to watch him putter around. He took a baking chicken from an earthen oven fashioned crudely in a corner and poked it once with a fork, then put it back again. An aroma told me there was more than the chicken in that rustic oven.

"It will be another ten or fifteen minutes," he said. "Let's have a drink. I want you to taste some home-brew and give me your honest opinion. I made it from the nectar of the mahua flower[7], not from rice. That stuff is too strong for me." With a smile, he took a bottle and two glasses from a shelf and motioned me to follow. We went out to the veranda and sat down with the glasses of home-brew in our hands.

"*Saluti,*" he toasted in his mother tongue. I sipped the thick liquid. It tasted both sweet and sour—and a bit muddy.

"Oh, no! It's terrible," the priest exclaimed. "Forgive me. It's not suited for a guest whom God so kindly has sent to me." He got up, took my glass, and went in again. In a few moments he reemerged, this time with a dusty, straw-covered bottle of Chianti.

"I thought I had drank my last bottle," he said. "But I found it. One last bottle, hidden behind the shelf. It survived without my knowledge, just for you." He looked very happy at the discovery.

We drank the first sip of Chianti as if it were nectar from heaven somehow available on earth. When he heard that I had been to many places in Italy, he was delighted. We toasted several times, remembering all the wonderful cities of his country. He began to tell me about the town where he was born.

"It's a little town called Monterchi, near Arezzo. When I was a boy, I remember, our milkman brought the milk in a cart pulled by a donkey. I can still hear the sound of the donkey's hooves on the cobblestones."

I told him how, on my first trip to Italy, I had ended up in Florence because I lost my Eurail pass on the train and a kind gentleman from Florence lent me money to buy a ticket; how this man put me up in his parents' *pensione* for a whole week until my money arrived. I told Father Angelo how eternally grateful I was to his countryman.

"Now, I am eternally grateful to *you*," he said, "for arriving in this God-forsaken place to help me drink my last bottle of Chianti. But, tell me, what exactly are you studying?"

"This place can't be so God-forsaken if you have found your way here," I said. "I'm studying the politics. What exactly are you doing here?" As soon as I asked this I felt ashamed and was about to apologize when he jumped from his chair and ran into

---

[7] The flower of the mahua tree is used to make a country wine. The tree is also valued for its timber and seed.

the house. Something was burning. I quickly followed him to the kitchen and saw him holding the partly-charred chicken. His face was filled with disappointment.

"But I like burnt food," I said. "Let's see how bad it is. We may be able to salvage something." I took the bird from his hand and brought it to the table to examine it. Father Angelo then took two loaves of bread from the oven, and these looked perfect. Only the chicken was affected. Deftly, he put the loaves in a basket, placing them on the table between two candles in wrought-iron holders. He lit the candles. We sat on either side of the rough-hewn table.

Father Angelo lowered his head slightly and said grace. He thanked God for bringing an unexpected guest to his humble home, for the overdone chicken, and for reminding him in time not to burn the bread as well. Inadvertently, I gave a muffled chuckle, and he, too, joined in. I looked up and saw in the candlelight a sprig of wild ginger blossom, in the same vase I had seen that morning on the linen-draped table in the clearing.

"When did you do all this?" I sputtered. "Cooking the chicken and setting the table? Weren't you making your rounds—holding services?" I paused, sensible of his efforts. "But the flower is lovely. Thank you, thank you so much."

"Oh, well, I picked the flowers when I came back briefly to put the chicken in the oven," he said. "There is a little valley not far from here where the wild ginger blooms like the narcissus in the fields of Umbria. I can show you the place." He is a genuinely good soul, I thought.

"But, you asked me before what I am doing here," he said softly. "I love this land, its rare beauty and its people who are so...so *uncontaminated,* compared to us, the Europeans." His voice was sad.

I could barely hear him. I looked at the candles, the glasses of wine, the two freshly-baked loaves of bread between us. I was again in a medieval town, the same town I had envisioned that morning. This time, I was taking part in a family meal. I was a member of a family of two, whose gods, languages, lands, were all far apart, yet mysteriously close. I felt welcome in this simple kitchen, eating Father Angelo's homemade bread and half-burnt chicken. I was so grateful to be with someone who took such care to make me feel at home in a place far from family and friends that my eyes filled with tears. Thank goodness Father Angelo was on the other side of the table and the flickering candles cast more shadow than light.

I did not know what time it was or how long we sat in silence. I saw a light through the window and soon heard footsteps outside. It was Tom, came to take me back to camp.

Then, as we all stood on the veranda, I realized that I had forgotten to ask Father Angelo for any information.

"Father," I said, "do you think you could introduce me to a Khasi headman in this area? In which case, I might delay leaving another day." I said all this before Tom could have a chance to object.

"Certainly," said the priest. "I can take you to one of the most powerful and controversial headmen for miles around. Why don't I come to your camp tomorrow at noon? Your driver can take us there."

Tom opened his mouth to say something.

"That sounds perfect," I said, quickly. "Thank you. I shall be ready." We walked toward the jeep, where Bahadoor sat waiting. Father Angelo shook hands with all of us and said good night.

"How exactly are we going to spend the whole day with this famous headman?" burst out Tom, once we were beyond earshot of the priest. "We have a schedule to keep. I have plans to be in Jampeng by two tomorrow. It's nearly *five* miles. I wish you consulted with me about these changes."

"Tom," I said, "I have interviews to conduct tomorrow morning. Then I'm meeting with the headman. No one is going anywhere until I'm done. You can help the cook break camp and pack, then arrange for departure by three. That should give us time to complete the trip to Jampeng by sundown, I'm sure." I surprised myself by my calm, firm tone. I supposed even Tom could not spoil the wonderful evening I had just spent.

— 1966 —

POLITICAL MAN

It had been densely foggy all morning, while I conducted the last interviews in the village of Lerkhla. Everything looked indistinct and ominous in the fog, and I was glad when I returned to the camp-site. Father Angelo arrived before noon to accompany me to the controversial headman. Bahadoor, Father Angelo, and I climbed into the jeep, waving goodbye to the sulking Tom, who was cleaning his betel-stained teeth with a neem twig[8]. The jeep moved slowly because of the poor visibility until, at one turn, it faced the south and the sun burst through the fog, dazzling our eyes.

"Look how lovely the view is in the noon sun!" said Father Angelo. The light hit his reddish beard, turning it bronze. At the sound of the jeep, two Khasi women by the roadside turned to look at us. They recognized the priest and smiled.

"Father," I said, "how do you explain the success of your church among the Khasi tribe?"

"I think it's the appeal of something new," he said. "And the figure of Christ is very appealing. A god who has a conceivable human form can be attractive to those who have had only supernatural beliefs." He smiled. "You're an anthropologist. You should know better than I."

"I think they are also impressed by the sacrifice and dedication of priests and missionaries like yourself," I said. "You came from thousands of miles away to live in these hills and jungles." I did not ask him what he had to say about the allegation that priests were mixing religion and politics. But he seemed to know my thoughts.

---

[8] From a bitter-tasting plant with medicinal properties.

"Some of your questions," he said, "may be answered better by the gentleman we are about to meet. Politics is something I do not understand well."

We had driven down into a small valley and soon came to a village. Father Angelo directed Bahadoor to stop in front of a house with a tin roof. Bahadoor stayed by the jeep, while Father Angelo and I went to the door.

We entered a room that looked like an office, except that the white-washed walls displayed a number of Khasi masks and handloomed fabrics. A man in his forties in a calf-skin jacket and blue jeans was reading an English newspaper. He looked up from the paper, folded it, and stood to greet us.

"Good morning, Father," he said to the priest. "You have departed from your routine today."

"Welcome to our land," he said to me. "I hear that you have come to study our people, to see what makes us tick. I see that you have found the right person to guide you. Father here knows where to find everything, including me. Please take a seat." The man showed no surprise at our unannounced visit to his office, and seemed to know a fair amount about me.

"Good morning. Thank you," I said, feeling a little ill at ease.

"Now that you are in the right hands," said Father Angelo to me, "I must be on my way. Thank you again for the surprise. Please come back, if you can."

He held my hand tightly for a moment. I was glad in a way that a stranger was present at this parting. It would not have been unlike me to indulge in sentimentality. I knew I might not see the warm-hearted priest again[9].

When we were alone, the headman again sat behind his desk. "Father Angelo is a very friendly man," he said. "He must have given you some ideas about us."

---

[9] In America, one evening twenty-five years after these events, I sat down to dinner with a group of people I had just met. A woman asked me where in India I was from. When I told her I had been born in Assam, she said that she knew of the area from a friend of her family, an Italian priest who lived there for many years. A few more details confirmed that it was indeeed Father Angelo. Then came the sad news: Father Angelo had died a few years before, in a hospital in America, where he had been moved by his church, of a disease he had contracted while working in the tropics.

"No, not really." I said. "He told me how much he likes this land and its people. He seems very dedicated." I picked up my notebook. "But I am here to listen to you. Tell me what you think about the conflict between the Khasis and the Nepalese."

A servant-boy brought a tray of tea cups and a pot covered with a colorful tea-cosy. It was very good Assam tea.

"Delicious," I said.

"Thank you. But soon we may not have much tea left, thanks to your government. And as for the Khasi-Nepali conflict, I believe it would never have happened if New Delhi had only taken certain measures. You see, your government rules us from a thousand miles' distance, knowing nothing about us." He put down his cup with a firm *clink*.

I saw that in his eyes I was practically a government agent—I was not a Khasi, and I came from the plains—and he needed someone upon whom to vent his anger. I felt like reminding him that I was only an objective observer, an anthropologist.

"Driving from Shillong a few weeks ago," I said, "I realized how far the Khasis really are from their own state capital, let alone from New Delhi. My bones are still aching from the ride over those dry riverbeds." Showing little interest in my aching bones, he lit a cigarette and continued his harangue.

"The central government will learn a tough lesson when the hill-tribes from all corners of this country start to rebel. Revolutionary ideas and up-to-date weapons are getting here from foreign countries, through Pakistan. They don't seem to require any paved roads. Even you could get here because you wanted to, right?"

"Yes," I answered. "I wanted to know more about the people and their politics. I was told you were the best person to enlighten me." This flattery seemed to distract the man for a moment. "I know what you are talking about," I continued. "I have already met at least a dozen young men, leaders of rural settlements who share your feelings—although they are not as articulate as yourself." These were the youths in trousers and leather jackets, educated in Shillong, who had returned to their villages to become teachers, leaders, and pastors.

"Can you blame them?" he said. "They know enough to see how neglected our people are by the government. If the authorities had paid some attention to the continuous flow of the

Nepalese into our land, the situation would not have gotten out of control. These people come here for our land—*and take it.*" He paused for a second to put his cigarette out vigorously.

"How exactly do the Nepalese do this?" I asked. "They cannot simply acquire your land without some sort of legal procedure." I was genuinely curious.

"Do you really want to know? They acquire the land by bribing bureaucrats in the state government. Simple as that. Oh, they will even produce the deeds—false documents, every one. Then they hire some of the poorer Khasis to plough the land. The Khasis are given paddy as wage—rice, not money. These poor fellows are also encouraged to make beer from the same paddy they have earned with hard labor. Once they take up such habits, there is no telling how much rice they will borrow from the employer." He took a long drag on the cigarette. "We Khasis are simple people, no match for these cunning Nepalese. It took us a while to get wise to their trickery."

"Excuse me," I said. "I'm a bit confused. Can one borrow grain like this? What methods are there for returning such loans?"

"Ha," he laughed, bitterly. "That's the tricky part. Of course they cannot return the grain they keep borrowing with compound interest. So they become permanently attached to their employers as debtors, not just as laborers. The Nepali employer thus receives free labor. The Khasi workers become poorer and up to their necks in debt for generations to come. In a few decades the whole Khasi nation will be ruined. You mark my words." The headman stopped. His brow quivered in anger. To compose himself, he lit another cigarette.

"And all this," he said, "could have been avoided if the high government officials had bothered to visit this area and see with their own eyes what was going on."

I began to feel very bad and almost as angry as the man in front of me. "Why doesn't someone like yourself go to Shillong in person and complain? I think this is unpardonable."

"Do you think they would listen? I'm a Khasi myself. They think I'm just being selfish and do not want to share my land with anyone else. Don't forget, these officials in Shillong have all been bribed by the wealthy Nepalese. The funds for the bribe, as you can guess, come from the same money they earn by exploiting my people."

I was very uncomfortable, not only because of these vivid tales of exploitation, but also because of my own reactions. Wasn't I supposed to avoid taking sides? Already I began to formulate in my mind a letter to the Minister of Tribal Affairs in New Delhi. I also began to dislike and perhaps to hate the Nepalese intruders, although I did consider the possibility that, as a Khasi, the headman might be exaggerating things.

Yet I was persuaded enough to take sides, despite my conscious efforts not to. Even back in Shillong where I had first heard about the situation, I had been inclined to sympathize with the Khasis. But now, I was breaking the cardinal law of "objectivity" in anthropological research. I felt guilty, and was eager to change the topic.

A diversion arrived in the form of a fresh pot of tea. I poured new cups for both of us.

"I'm terribly sorry about all this," I ventured. "I shall try my best to inform my colleagues about what is happening here. But, as you know, we are only research people and have very little political power."

"You have more power than we have at such a distance," he returned. "I'm sure your colleagues in Calcutta or New Delhi would listen to you more closely than the officials in Shillong listen to me."

"Possibly." I put aside my cup and stood up to examine one of the masks. "Tell me about the Khasi social system. I am especially curious about the women. I've been observing how hard they work. Do you find it odd that yours is one of the few matrilineal societies left in the world?"

The topic of women seemed to distract the man from his political interests. For the first time since I arrived, he smiled. Stretching his legs in front of him, he leaned his head back a little and exhaled a perfect smoke-ring.

"Of course, you wish to know about the women. They are very powerful in this country. They own the land, and the youngest daughter in a family usually stays with the parents and takes care of them as they grow older. Her husband has very little say about this. The poor fellow."

"Obviously you haven't married a youngest daughter."

"Oh, no," he said. "I'm not married right now. Women nowadays are not trustworthy. Do you know that the primary reason for our high divorce rate is adultery among women?" He seemed eager to discuss this, as if it were a new target upon which to vent his anger.

"I see," I returned. "But with whom exactly do these women commit adultery?" There was a pause. The headman burst out laughing. We both laughed. The atmosphere of complaint was evaporating. I looked at my watch. I really needed to get back to the topic I had come to discuss.

"I fully agree with you," I said, taking a different tack, "about the predicament of your people and also about the total neglect by the central government. Believe me, we in the plains aren't any happier with the government, either."

The headman shifted in his rattan chair, which he then pulled forward a bit, and began to talk with intensity. I saw Bahadoor through the window beyond; but seeing us so involved, he moved away. For the next ten minutes I heard much more about the political situation. I learned how some of the newly-imposed tariffs interfered with the headman's own interests along the border which separated the state from the eastern part of Pakistan[10]. The cut in his income from the markets on the border was a big blow, although ideas and smuggled goods could still pass unnoticed. For the first time I saw that he was using a West German cigarette lighter. He must be keeping the border guards happy by bribing them, I thought. He understood the meaning of my gaze.

"I am not concerned about the smuggling of little luxury goods such as this," he said. He tossed the lighter from one hand to the other. "The real problem is the change in the customs rules without any consideration for the local population. It is hard to keep up with all the details. So I keep running back and forth between the District Council in Shillong and the Khasi Darbar—our own body of administrators, headed by my mother's brother."

I realized that surely, given the authentic blue blood running back through all his ascending generations, he held a trump card

---

[10] Once part of Pakistan, this area became the independent republic of Bangladesh in 1971.

for swaying public opinion. He would no doubt himself be elected a member of the District Council someday.

He had stopped, perhaps a little exhausted from the long litany of complaint. He looked out through the open door at the distant hills. The sun was high in the sky. There were no shadows on the slopes now, where occasional boulders of quartz glittered like silver.

"Aren't you happy to be in this beautiful country of mine?" he asked, in a very different tone. I could only smile, in affirmation and sympathy.

"Thank you for your time," I said. "I have learned a lot. I wish you all the luck in your struggles, not only against the Nepalese, but also with the government."

"Thank you for listening. Perhaps you can help in some way." He extended his hand toward me and shook mine warmly.

"Perhaps," I said.

I could see Bahadoor waiting patiently in the shade of a tree.

— *1966* —

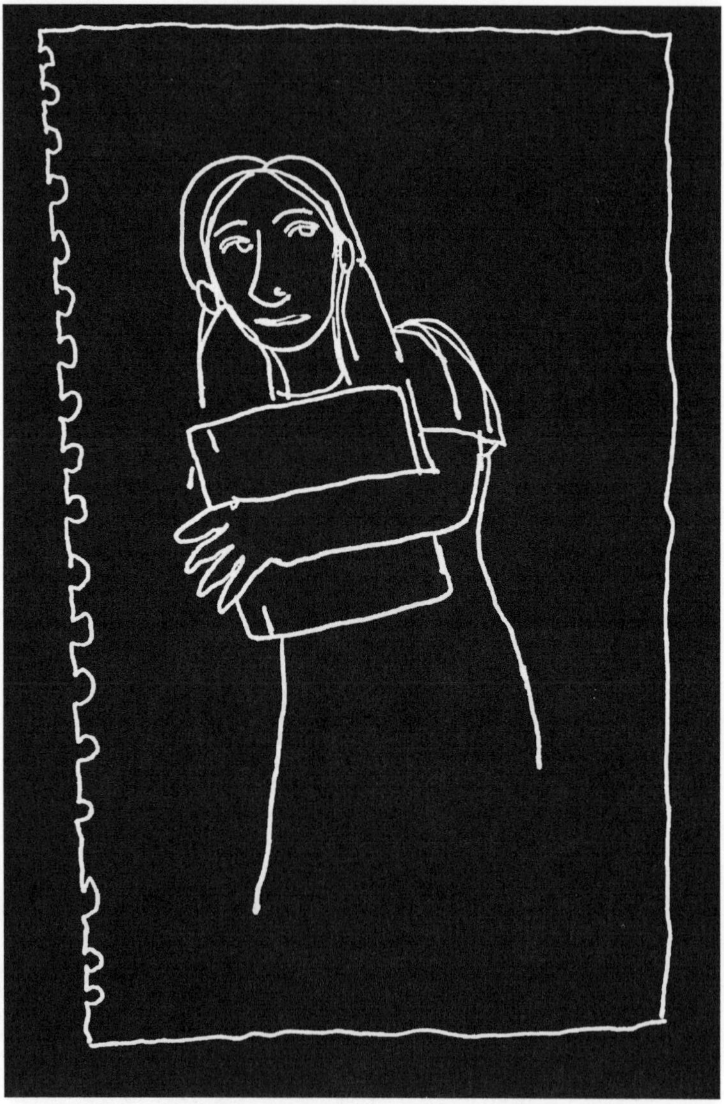

A Schoolteacher's Daughter

When I first approached Sohliya, some forty miles east of the Khasiland, I noticed a difference in both the landscape and the houses. It is a Miri village at the very fringe of the Mikir Hills. The Miris are a hill-tribe who live near the nontribal Assamese people of the plains and borrow freely from the latter's way of life. Their houses, like those of the Khasis, are made of bamboo, but are more spacious, and often have an attached granary. The granary, a conical structure like a giant palm-leaf hat, sits well above the ground, on pilings, to protect it from nocturnal animals.

The Miris have a distinct language, though many speak Assamese as well, in order to conduct trade with their neighbors. On arrival, I felt somewhat at ease, given my familiarity with Assamese; but this familiarity, I soon learned, also bore its share of limitations.

I had hitched a ride in a government vehicle to a market square in the village that afternoon, and was left there to fend for myself. This was to be a "control" exercise, in which I would gather information about a hill-tribe other than the Khasis. Ostensibly, the information would also be of use in New Delhi.

I found the Miris not as hospitable toward me as the Khasis had been. There were fewer bows and smiles in their greetings. I was not an exotic newcomer, nor even the first anthropologist to set foot in the village. Moreover, they had no difficulty placing me as a Bengali who had some knowledge of the Assamese language. Their Assamese neighbors, with whom they were on good terms, had a long-standing ambivalence toward the Bengalis and this now made me look a bit suspect to them. It was up to me to earn their friendship. As usual, I decided to take the plunge, with hope for quick rapport and the subsequent smooth fieldwork.

Nevertheless, within an hour of my arrival, it appeared that either my Assamese was inadequate or the Miris were pretending not fully to understand me. Then, after much difficult negotiation, I was told there was no place for me to stay.

Since I had had no need of an interpreter, I was able up to this point to do without Tom, my Khasi assistant. Now I wished he were here, his relentless talk notwithstanding. He would use the powers of his salesmanship to find me a place for the night. Alone, I had no such powers.

It would be dark soon. The Miris told me in their Assamese, which I understood perfectly, that no one had informed them that I would be spending nights in their village. They were under the impression that I was to visit them during the day and return to the nearest Assamese village, four miles away, every evening. What they must have thought of anthropologists!

As a professional with an official purpose, who had entered the area for the first time, I knew I had to obtain the approval of the significant males of the village. Thus I was talking entirely to men. I now wondered if the women would feel differently if they knew my predicament. The few women in sight were busy pounding paddy and sweeping the yards, or gathering up the children and animals, the usual activities before a day's end in these villages. Now I was getting nervous. If only I could find a Mother Lyndoh here....

To my surprise, one of the men volunteered to accompany me on foot to the Assamese village. He was to go there that evening if he were to attend a market early the next morning. But walking four miles in the dark with a stranger did not seem a realistic option. That I must speak with him a language neither of us spoke well was no advantage. I would be a fool to accept this offer knowing how the paths looked at night. Besides, the moon was long waning; there would be no light. And I had a briefcase to carry. Even if I could trust the man, I was sure to break an ankle or step on some dangerous creature crawling in or out of its hole alongside the path.

I was about to give up hope (and the facade of the self-sufficient scholar and adventurer) when an elderly woman brought me a drink in a small bamboo mug. I sipped it through a thin reed straw; I liked the taste. Perhaps this kind woman will help me, I thought. But she appeared unaware of my problems.

My enthusiasm revived because of the drink, which was a home-brewed millet beer. Warm water is mixed with millet in the bamboo mug to produce a mild fermentation. I had tasted a similar brew in other parts of the hills of Assam, and in Sikkim[11] and Nepal, when I was there in my college days. It was not enough to allay my present anxiety, however, although I did become less polite. I urged them to provide me a corner of a mat in some household for the night.

Their lack of hospitality might have had something to do with their notion of an educated woman's capabilities. If I could go all the way to America to study, they might have thought, I should be able to navigate four miles of hilly paths in the dark. So, at least, I reasoned, I could be faithful to this image of a female anthropologist and make the hike. I suppose the millet beer might have helped me to reach this foolhardy decision. Looking back, I really had no choice.

My companion, a stocky man of about thirty, began to walk on ahead of me, while I thanked the woman who had been kind enough to provide the millet beer—though not a shelter for the night. I started walking, determined not to set foot in this unfriendly village again. For the next quarter of an hour, I thought that I might not be cut out to be an anthropologist after all. I could not even charm a few villagers to put me up for the night. In my frustration, I had failed to notice that my guide had a small lantern and was holding it behind him every minute or two. Now I felt grateful.

"Thank you," I said. He fell back a bit, keeping abreast in the narrow path whenever possible. I resolved to strike up a conversation and make it easier for both of us. I had heard somewhere that if one talked even a potential enemy softened, though I had no reason to be suspicious of this benefactor.

"What is your name?" I asked.

"Diburu," he said. He then told me about himself in a mix of Miri and Assamese. I thus heard his story in bits and pieces, interspersed with the sound of our steps and the occasional call of some night bird. The rattle of crickets was constant and high-pitched. I strained to hear him, while keeping my eyes on the narrow path visible only in the intermittent light of his lantern.

---

[11] Once a sovereign Himalayan principality, this area became a protectorate of India in 1950 and a state of India in 1975.

Diburu had been an orphan, brought up by a poor aunt. The aunt was kind but had not the strength to fight with her husband and keep Diburu for very long. The husband resented feeding an extra mouth. So when he was ten, Diburu left home and went down to the plains to look for jobs in the more liberal Assamese households. He worked as a servant-boy in several homes until he was old enough to become a porter, which paid more. He became independent.

At this point in his story, and in the path, he paused. I was so interested in hearing more that I would have urged him to continue. But I waited. I looked up, as if to see his face. There was only shadow. The dusty smell of the path now mingled with the vegetal odor of the vines and trees. It was an odor I had experienced many times before: that of a tropical forest at night. I had long associated the smell of a forest at night with an inner, unnamed anxiety—and, likewise, with a curiosity I was powerless to deny. In my mind now, I saw vines wrapping the bamboo and other trees as a python wraps its prey. I saw moss dripping from the branches. Would I now encounter something unexpected? Something dangerous? I then saw in the shadows to our left the faint hint of another path.

"Memsahib, the road is very difficult," said Diburu in his broken Assamese. "If you wish, there is a house nearby where we might spend the night. It is the house of my friend, a young woman. Her village is less than a mile from here, and it is not uphill. We could make it easily."

This surprised me very much. Was it a rendezvous? I looked at the young man next to me, as well as I could in the soft light of the lantern, which he now held before us. He seemed very ordinary and not so young, not at all my idea of a man who had a woman waiting for him at the edge of the forest. But then, why not? Such a notion only revealed my own prejudice as to what romance and love ought to be. I was again very interested. I relaxed for the first time since we began our trek. A man in love would not harm another woman, I reasoned. Without further hesitation, I accepted the change of plan. I was tired of stumbling along the dark and narrow path.

In half an hour we found ourselves in front of a little hut, neatly tucked away, such as one encounters in a dream or a fairy tale. Diburu's friend, to my amazement, was a young Assamese who spoke perfect English and appeared totally urbanized. I could not tell if I had to thank the unfriendly village of Sohliya—or my own good luck—for handing up such a situation, for having led me where smooth and well-planned fieldwork could never go.

We ate a lovely meal of chicken curry and rice. Afterward, while Diburu waited in one room, the young woman and I settled back in the other, with our legs tucked under a handwoven blanket. She then told me her story.

Her name was Phutukoni. She was born in a small town about a hundred miles south of this area and lower in elevation. Her father was a school teacher—a headmaster—with a modest income. She, the eldest of three sisters, was the father's favorite because of her interest in her studies even as a child. The father made special arrangements with the authorities to have his daughters admitted to the all-boys school where he was headmaster, and the girls went to school with him every day. The father helped them with their homework.

The daughters were brought up under strict care. Their mother did not quite agree with her husband's enthusiasm for educating them. She had heard the same stories years before about his college days that he now told every evening to his daughters.

The headmaster instilled a stronger sense of the adventure of learning in his eldest daughter than he did in the other two. As a child, Phutukoni saw that learning was more important than anything else in life. She wanted to know more about everything and felt a zest for knowledge. She adored her father.

When Phutukoni graduated from high school, her mother began hinting about a marriage negotiation. The headmaster would ignore any such suggestion. He was an idealist. The brightest of his daughters must have at least a couple of years of college, that wonderfully enriching experience, which he still considered the most valuable asset of his own life.

"After a bachelor's degree, she could end her bachelorhood," he punned in English to his wife.

One day, while Phutukoni was waiting for her admission to college, the headmaster came home with Diburu the porter, who was carrying a heavy desk. Diburu stayed for a meal, which was customary to offer for such services. In the afternoon, when Phutukoni wandered through the garden picking flowers, she saw the Miri man helping her father to gather coconuts from a tree. She knew a few words in Miri. She asked him the name of his village. Did he have a family? Diburu burst out laughing. He told her that she had asked him if he would like to make her his family! Phutukoni was embarrassed, but laughed with him. She was drawn to this uneducated tribal man for his unabashed manners, his hearty laugh, and for something else she could not name. Diburu had nothing in common with her or her dreams for the future. Her zest for knowledge had nothing to do with this man who worked as a porter and lived an unlettered, simple life.

Phutukoni asked her father to employ Diburu in the house so that she could give him a few lessons in reading and arithmetic. The headmaster was very pleased to see that his daughter was rapidly becoming a teacher. He was proud that she was willing to teach someone who had no opportunity to go to school. The parents, of course, did not suspect anything until much later, when one day Phutukoni told them that she loved Diburu and wanted to marry him. Even the headmaster found it impossible to approve of such an unlikely match, idealist or not.

Phutukoni left home. It had been a year now. She became a social worker and moved to this little village not far from the Miri territory. Her parents had tried to dissuade her, but she said she would not return home until they accept Diburu as their son-in-law.

So, Pygmalion in reverse, I thought.

"The strange thing is, Diburu is not at all interested in learning to read or write—or in any such thing, for that matter," said Phutukoni, sensing the nature of my thoughts. "I'm not sure he even needs it. You know, sometimes he puts me to shame with all his knowledge of trees, birds, and animals. All the books I have read never taught me the things he knows: how to laugh and live and love. I love him because he is more of a surprise to me than a book could ever be. He proves to me that to live, to love, to be human, one does not need books or schools."

"Quite a statement," I said, "coming from a headmaster's daughter who believed in learning and books so much herself."

"Don't you think," I added, with some hesitation, "that your education has something to do with your independence, and with your courage to love a man like Diburu?"

"Oh, I don't know," said Phutukoni. "Diburu respects me for my education. He says so. But he is not envious. He does not wish to be like me. He knows how much I admire him for his natural intelligence. He is so simple and good. Perhaps education would destroy that goodness. I really don't know." This indirect response to my question suggested the existence of a problem that was still unclear to her.

"What about the future?" I asked. "Do you think you would be able to marry him and be accepted by his family, his tribe? Can you bear the guilt of defying your family, your culture, for the rest of your life?" It was odd that I could ask her so bluntly. But something about her made it possible.

"I have thought about it," she responded. "Right now I am not worried about the future. I'm quite happy the way things are. Diburu wants a child, so we think about marrying soon. Perhaps we will go to Shillong or to some big city where no one knows us. So long as we love and respect each other, I do not worry. As for my family, I'm sure that someday they will come to see Diburu for who he really is. I trust my father's judgment. He will recognize Diburu's qualities. He taught me to be who I am."

What, I wondered, about the need to communicate on a more educated level with her husband? But somehow this very obvious question seemed irrelevant.

"It's getting late," said Phutukoni. "You need your rest. I'll see you in the morning." She went to the other room, where Diburu was waiting for her.

I stretched out on the bed where we had been talking for the last hour. It had been a long, eventful day. I was tired but not sleepy. Many thoughts were crowding my mind: Is Phutukoni exceptional? Is Diburu? Are there many cultures that give rise to individuals like Phutukoni or Diburu? Are people like them found only in a very small village nobody knows about? Or can they be found anywhere? What exactly is the connection between moral courage and education? Is it only love that makes a twenty-year-old woman so brave as to defy her whole culture?

A vague realization that these were *my* questions, not Phutukoni's, is all I can remember further of that night. Sleep took me far from my ponderings.

— 1966 —

When I returned to Shillong from the field, it became clear that my stay in the area would soon end. Circumstances at the Anthropological Survey office made it impossible for me to return to the field alone. To my great annoyance, a male colleague had begun to show undue interest in my private life. And before any consultation with me, he got permission from our supervisors to accompany me on my next trip to the field. When I objected, with the argument that I would be safer alone than with someone like him, neither my boss in Shillong nor the superiors in Calcutta seemed to appreciate the gravity of the situation. When all my appeals failed, I had no choice but to resign and go back to Calcutta. For the next year I funded and conducted my own fieldwork in West Bengal, where I knew the language and had enough contacts to stay within the protection of established families. The first four pieces in this section were written during this period—upon my return to Shillong, and then in West Bengal—in 1966 and 1967.

People Of The Plains

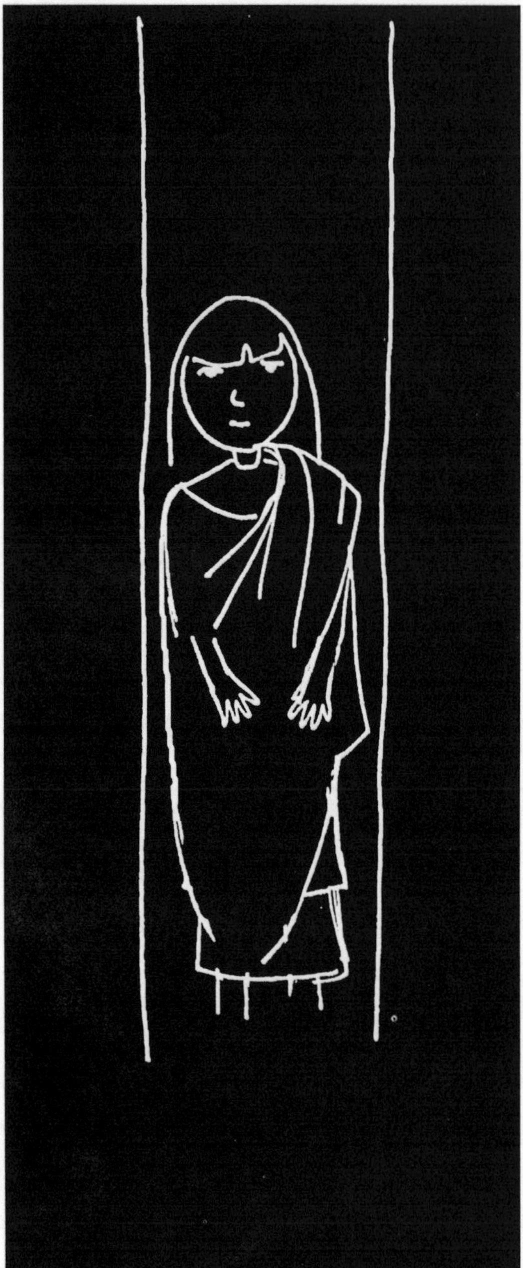

At Sunset

The monsoon season arrived and I returned to Shillong from the Khasi Hills. But the feeling grew within me that my work there was not finished. I saw that I needed to go back, if not to the same area, then to somewhere nearby it. I had not yet gotten under the surface of the culture and its people.

I had already arranged to return to Calcutta and begin work in the villages of West Bengal. My plan was to gather enough data to make a comparative study of the hill and the plains peoples. Then, suddenly, when the feeling of unfinished work in Assam most possessed me, an opportunity for action presented itself.

At a party one day I met a few government officials who had contacts with the local-level politicians in a town called Rahabari, near Nowgong, which is about seventy miles northeast of Shillong. It was in Assam, but between the hills and the plains.

I wanted to discuss the change of plan with someone and I chose Professor Bose for this, not anyone at the Anthropological Survey, which I was soon to leave. The professor supported my decision, but offered a word of caution. "This time," he wrote, "you will study a group closer in kind to your own culture, whose language you can speak. This may be a disadvantage. You may not meet with the interest and respect accorded to a stranger. Yet you are Bengali; therefore, an outsider. Keep this in mind. Don't try to teach the Assamese ladies to cook fish curry in the Bengali way. They may not like that."

After a four-hour train ride to Nowgong late one morning, I got on a commuter bus for Rahabari. I had no idea so many kinds of people used this means of transportation. The bus was severely overcrowded. Before I could reach a rail from which to cling, I had stumbled up the aisle past a row of squatting, kneeling children and over several baskets of live chickens and large bundles of betel leaves tied with scratchy ropes. The bus driver gave me no time to find so much as a foothold. I fell, and crushed something which emitted a loud, percussive groan. Somehow I managed to right myself and apologize to the owner of the musical instrument. It was covered by a long pillow case, into which its owner now stared.

What a journey! When my hour as a tinned sardine was ended and I found my way to the door, I did not mind so much the pushes and scratches this time, although I was sorry to leave the conversation with the musician. It had been very interesting.

It was a relief to breathe fresh air again, after the mixed human and animal odors of the bus. A young man of twenty-five or so greeted me with a broad smile and joined palms, in one of which was cupped a cigarette.

"I am the son of Mr. Sharma, who is delighted to be your host for as long as you wish." His silk shirt, smooth skin, and highly-refined manners displayed the breeding of an aristocrat, though with the hint of a rural origin. His smile displayed tobacco-stained teeth.

"How kind of you to meet me," I said, as Mr. Sharma, Junior, led me to a bicycle-rickshaw.

"Not only is my family honored to welcome you," he said, "but I myself am particularly happy because I have always been interested in anthropology. I shall be glad to offer any assistance you may require while you are here. By the way, your Assamese is sweet because of your American accent."

I was grateful to him for putting me at ease by this superfluous compliment; my Assamese was barely adequate. "Thank you," I said. "And thank you for the offer. I may take you up on it."

My first hour at the Sharma's was spent in the front room of their two-storey brick house, having tea with Mr. Sharma, Senior, and three other men of rather vague identity. The gentleman with polished shoes, who occupied the mahogany chair, was some sort of leader of the local Congress Party. The other two, on the little bench, were villagers who frequented this household to ask for favors or merely to sit around. I had seen this phenomenon in villages all over India: wealthy landlords surrounded by casual visitors whose sole purpose is to spend time in the presence of a powerful man.

"How honored I am," said Mr. Sharma, welcoming me warmly, "to be the host to such a learned woman of my country!"

He took a puff on his hookah. "My daughter Rani has finished her college degree and is now a schoolteacher. I hope she can follow in your footsteps some day." Puffing noisily once more upon the pipe, he signaled the servant-boy to take my bags inside.

"Go, call Rani-didi to come here."

For a man of sixty or sixty-five, Mr. Sharma appeared quite well-built, although portly. An air of importance surrounded his manners. His beak-like nose hung over his tight lips, reminding me of an eagle. His eyes were slightly red, but kind.

The servant-boy, who had been preparing the tobacco for the hookah, staring at me all the while, got up and disappeared through the curtain that separated the outer house from the inner. Mr. Sharma made a remark to one of the men about a politician. My attention drifted a bit until the daughter appeared at the door, drawing aside the curtain and stepping into the room.

I was struck by the upright gait of the soft-skinned young woman. She can hardly be twenty, I thought. But there was something troubling in her almond-shaped eyes.

"This is my daughter Rani," said Mr. Sharma to me. Rani did not look at me directly.

"Take your new sister inside," he said to her, "and introduce her to your mother and the others. Also, see that she is made comfortable. Is her room ready?"

Rani nodded her head slightly and walked away, leading me into the inner house. We entered the kitchen, where her mother, a fair-skinned, chubby woman with slightly grey, oily hair, was sitting on a cane stool giving instructions to the cook. When I touched the mother's feet in a greeting of respect, Bengali-fashion, she seemed very pleased, and welcomed me by uttering the popular blessing, "Live long and be a mother of many sons."

That afternoon, after lunch and a refreshing nap, I thought how lucky I was to happen upon a family like this. At last I would be in a situation to conduct some solid fieldwork. I loitered in bed making mental notes about my schedule for the next day. Rani walked in without knocking, which did not surprise me. She seemed to be a bit odd, and independent at the same time. She asked whether I would like to have tea with the rest of the family or alone in my room. I was pleased to hear that I had a choice in the matter.

"Why don't we, the two of us, have tea on the roof terrace?" I suggested. Rani was visibly pleased, and we soon climbed the narrow steps to the roof, where we could almost touch the tops of the coco palms that surrounded the house. We sat on mats on the moss-covered mortar floor with the tea-tray between us. Everything seemed as perfect and comfortable as the cool green carpet beneath our feet.

"You must help me, Manishadi," said Rani. "I don't know who else to turn to. I need your help desperately." The anxiety in her voice was real enough to shake me out of the comfort of the moment before. She then told me a most disturbing tale.

Rani had fallen in love with a colleague, another teacher in her school, three years before. She did not tell anyone anything for the first year, thinking that it would pass, because there was no chance of marriage. Her family would never agree to a marriage with someone who was not a Brahmin[12]. When, after two years, she realized that she was more involved than ever, she broke the news—first to her mother, who was always more understanding. Nevertheless, no amount of persuasion by her mother could change her father's views. Her mother then urged her to forget the young man or she would have to leave her job and stay at home until they found an appropriate match for her. She agreed to this, but struggled with herself for a year. She saw that she could not stop loving the man. Now, she found herself pregnant.

In a way, she had been waiting for her parents to change their minds. But the predicament now was more than she could handle. She had not told anyone about the pregnancy except her lover. She felt it was God's blessing that I arrived when I did.

"You must help me with a doctor's name in Calcutta," she implored, "where I can go and have an abortion without anyone knowing."

Rani's eyes were full of tears as she clutched my hands in appeal. I was taken aback, not so much by the story of her love and pregnancy, but by her trust—and by her demand for help. She had barely met me. I had been told that my being an outsider

---

[12] (Also spelled Brahman.) In Hindu India, the highest in rank of the four varnas, or castes, originally—in late Vedic India—the priestly class.

could play to some advantage in my work, but this! Knowing rural India, I could see how desperate her situation was. But how could I help her even if I had no compunction about abortion? It would be ungrateful to the family who had given me such hospitality were I to assist her. And there were other things to consider: my work, my future. The breeze through the palm leaves suddenly felt uncomfortable. I told her the only thing I could: I would think about it.

"Didi," she said, touching my feet as she spoke, "I realize what a difficult thing I'm asking of you. I see no other way. I am more willing to live with the guilt of killing my child than to pull my family down into the mud. I know now that I must sacrifice the baby and my love to protect the family name. Perhaps, someday, if I serve my parents and never marry, God will forgive me this crime."

"What about your boyfriend?" I asked. "What does he say? Aren't you two better off going away and settling somewhere in the city where no one knows you?" I was thinking of another young woman as I spoke. Yet I saw the futility of the suggestion as soon as I made it. She was not Phutukoni.

"My boyfriend docs not think it's a good idea to elope," she said. "We've discussed it already. He thinks that we would never be happy if we bore the curse of having betrayed the honor of our families. I agree with him."

Night was falling. The mosquitoes began their rounds. Rani collected the tea-things. It was sunset, time for her to go down and blow the conch-shell announcing the evening, like all the Hindu girls in the village. As I followed her down the narrow steps, I assured her again that I would think about her problem.

That night I lay awake, wondering about my luck, which had begun to run out rapidly. Something in me did not want to think at all about the whole situation. It was too soon for me to face such a problem, coming before I had had a chance to enjoy my good fortune a bit. I was annoyed with Rani for stealing that from me. In the dark of night my thoughts were selfish.

A day passed. I busied myself with the initial logistics of my research. Questions and concerns about Rani gnawed at me from time to time. Upon nightfall, they came crowding. Many of these questions had little relevance at that point. Why hadn't Rani or her boyfriend used any precaution? Contraceptives are available everywhere in India. And how was my educated, liberal outlook going to help me find a way to help her? But before I had fully formulated these questions, I knew the answer. I knew I could not do anything. I also knew the reasons why I could not.

Wasn't I trained to be a participant observer? It was the "participant" part that was not at all clear. I was participating in this household as a guest. The Sharmas took me in with open arms. Not only had Rani's father referred to me as her sister, but she herself had called me so. If all this happened to my own sister, wouldn't I help her? Was my dilemma only a professional one? Could I dismiss the whole issue of the family honor because of my Western education? What would I do if *I* were—? I did not want to go on and on with these endless questions.

I rose next morning after a sleepless night. My first thought was whether I were the only anthropologist to face this particular dilemma. No books on fieldwork had ever mentioned anything like this.

I decided to escape all the worry by getting busy. I needed to line up some appointments with political leaders and census offices. I would also need, at some point, to find an assistant to perform simple office tasks for me. I thought of Rani. It would be perfect for her, I thought; it would take her away from her brooding for a little while. I must find a way to pay her so that we could keep this totally separate from our relationship. Later, we will come up with some sort of solution to her crisis.... My problems, and hers, seemed less complicated in the clear light of day. Or was I getting more professional and less involved?

I did not see Rani for a few days. Is she avoiding me, I wondered, or is she giving me more time? When I asked for her I was told that she was at school or at the neighbors'. I saw a lot of the junior Mr. Sharma, but could not tell if he had any knowledge of his sister's situation. Either he had no idea or he was being very discreet. She said she had not told anyone else.

After dinner one evening, Rani showed up at my door. She sat on the edge of my bed where I was lying with a book. She waited quietly for me to speak, looking at me with sad but questioning eyes.

"Rani," I said. "I just cannot come up with the name of a doctor in Calcutta who would be willing to perform an abortion. I need more time to think, please." My words sounded empty.

"Don't worry," I felt compelled to add, "together we will find a solution. Meanwhile, I won't tell anyone anything. Your secret is safe with me." Rani said nothing at first. As she looked at me, I had the feeling she could see through me despite her tearful eyes.

"I don't know how to show you my gratitude, Manishadi," she said. "Someday I will repay you."

I lay on my bed a long time after she left. My "lies" were keeping me from sleep, as had my questions a few days earlier.

Another week passed. To avoid thinking of the problem, I made myself busier than ever.

One evening I returned at sunset from a neighboring village where I had discovered a census office with much useful information. I decided to ask Rani if she would like to help by copying out some of the data. Or, I thought, should I look for someone outside the family to do the job? When I stepped out of the bicycle-rickshaw, the house looked completely dark. That was very unusual. I managed to climb the stairs to the second floor. Then I heard the sound of sobbing, coming from Rani's mother's room. I could see the maids in the dim hallway, standing with their saris pressed to their eyes, crying. One of them told me that Rani's body had been found in the well late that afternoon, when one of the servants had gone there to draw water.

I ran downstairs again. I wanted one of the servants to take me to the burning ghat. I was told it was ten miles away; it would perhaps be finished. The family would be on their way back soon....

I had managed to remain uninvolved after all. A pair of tearful, almond-shaped eyes haunted me for many nights to come. I left the Sharmas' very soon after the tragedy and never finished the work I had begun in Rahabari, the work that had looked so promising. The unfinished work of the Khasi Hills remained unfinished after all.

Rani, I have told your secret.

— 1967 —

The Beggarwoman of Calcutta

In the residential section of South Calcutta, at the corner of Lansdowne Road and an unnamed lane, is a little shop that supplies the neighborhood with such things as candy, betel, and cigarettes, and with small amounts of sugar, tea, and flour. My aunt's house is across the lane, on the corner opposite the shop, and faces the wide Lansdowne Road. From her second-floor balcony, one can look out over a flurry of cars and double-decker buses, of rickshaws and bicycles—or out over the lane, to the little grey storefront. My aunt uses the shop only for emergencies, when one child or another is sent down to fetch a quarter-pound of loose tea or a half-pound of sugar.

I had forgotten about the little shop until I went back to Calcutta after six years of study in America and several months of research in the hills of Assam. I was staying with my aunt for a couple of weeks before going out to the villages of West Bengal for fieldwork.

"What exactly is it that you will be doing in the villages?" she asked one morning at the breakfast table. "What is anthropology?" Her questions took me by surprise. I struggled to find words that would not sound academic.

"Well," I said, "I shall observe and record the activities of people throughout the day, and ask them questions about why they do what they do, if possible. I may also study their institutions, such as marriage and the caste system. Then I will write a report about their lives that may contribute something to the literature of anthropology, which simply means 'the study of people'."

"I see," she said, when she had taken this in. For a moment I thought she didn't approve of anthropology. Then a gleam came to her eyes. "Why don't you study this neighborhood here? You will be surprised how much you can do on this corner alone." She gestured to the window. The gleam was getting brighter.

"Why don't you observe the beggars who live on the street below? They are an institution by themselves. Why bother to go all the way to the villages? Here, at least you have an aunt to look after you."

I saw that my aunt wanted to keep me with her for as long as she could, but I was not sure how serious she was about what I could observe on the street.

"Would it be valuable, do you think?" I asked her.

She crossed to the balcony and pointed to the little shop across the lane. "If you watch what goes on there for a few days, you will know what I mean."

So, the next day, I began an unplanned observation from my aunt's balcony, in the style of "Rear Window."

At about five a.m., when the first bus went by and the old milkman brought his cow to be milked in front of the buyers of the lane, I saw an old woman crawl from an opening beneath the shop. A tattered palm-leaf mat covered the opening, whose recesses could not have been more than six feet by eight feet— and only four feet in height. She moved slowly down the lane to a place near a hydrant to relieve herself. Meanwhile, a younger woman, perhaps in her late twenties, came out of the same mat-covered opening with a small charcoal burner and lit it, fanning the coals with folded newspapers. For the morning tea, she put water on the burner in a used shortening can.

One by one the whole family came out from under the shop. There were five of them in all. They sat on the pavement and drank black tea from small plastic cups. The older woman and the two children—aged no more than ten—got some puffed rice to go with their tea. I noticed the young woman served tea to the older woman, and then helped her to move away from the roadside and sit in the first warm rays of the rising sun.

"Her name is Kuruni. See how she serves her mother-in-law first," my aunt whispered. I hadn't noticed I had company on the balcony.

When the family finished their breakfast, Kuruni (a word that means "scavenger") drank whatever tea was left. She washed the can and the cups in the muddy water from the hydrant. Then they set off on their rounds. The husband and the elder child, a boy, left in one direction and Kuruni and the little girl took off in another, passing under our balcony. My aunt and I went in to have our breakfast.

My aunt told me that Kuruni's husband was a pickpocket and a part-time thief. One day he and the shopkeeper had a fight over the rent of the space under the shop. The shopkeeper threatened that he would tell the police about the husband's activities if he did not pay the five rupees[13] rent every month. The husband shouted in reply that he himself could report the shopkeeper, who was not supposed to rent such an unlivable space to anyone.

The maid joined in the conversation, telling me that it was common knowledge how these people earned their living. The father and son went to the nearest market, where the crowd was heaviest between six and seven. They did not pick pockets then because the servants carried the shopping money in the folds of their lungis and dhotis[14], not in the pockets of shirts and pants. The little boy made a few rupees carrying the shopping bags of one woman or fetching a rickshaw for another. After the market the father and son would part company. Apparently, the man chose the busiest bus-stops for his most lucrative business. My aunt continued the story when the maid went down to do the washing.

At noon, Kuruni would come home with a small basket of rice, lentils, vegetable trimmings, and a fish tail or the feathered remnants of a chicken. She had made the rounds of affluent homes to beg, displaying her little daughter's skeletal body. She usually managed to collect enough grain and food-stuffs for at least two meals, thanks to the guilt and compassion of the middle-class housewives. Occasionally, Kuruni did not return till late in the afternoon. She might then have got a bite for herself and her daughter in some house or other.

By now I was drawn totally into the life and whereabouts of Kuruni's family. I pulled a chair up to a window, watching for anything to happen throughout the afternoon; it was too sunny on the balcony that time of day. Nothing happened, except once or twice I caught sight of the boy playing in the lane with a few other children.

---

[13] In 1966, approximately one U.S. dollar.
[14] A lungi is a cylindrical garment stitched close at the waist; a dhoti is a long loincloth that wraps around the hips and thighs.

Just as I finished my afternoon tea, my aunt pointed in the direction of the shop. I carried my cup to the balcony thinking that my aunt was rapidly becoming a better research assistant than the one who worked for me in Assam.

I positioned myself in a way so that no one from below could suspect my motives. I even had a newspaper to hide my face, just in case. The Lansdowne Road was very busy and noisy this time of day. Overcrowded buses moved through a tangle of other vehicles and through a swarm of rickshaws, bicycles, and pedestrians. At sundown, the street lamps intensified the dusty winter smog. I could barely make out what was going on in front of the little shop.

Kuruni returned with her daughter, carrying a basket covered with a dirty cloth. They looked haggard from the day's errands. I wondered what the mother-in-law did all day. As if in response, she appeared from behind the mat as she had done that morning. Kuruni made tea again, then squatted down to prepare the family's evening meal. From what I could make out, she cooked a gruel with the things she collected from begging, and served it to the mother-in-law and the children. All these activities took place right at the roadside, among the milling crowds of the lane. No one seemed to notice.

I was not able to watch the beggar family again until later in the evening. Everything was quiet then. Kuruni was sitting next to the shop on an old cane stool. She was waiting for her husband, I presumed. He came late, after the last bus had left, bringing fried cakes in a cone of old newspapers. Together they ate and chatted for a while. I wondered if he were telling her the day's adventures in his forbidden profession. The light of his *bidi*, the country-style cigarette[15], flickered awhile in the shadows, even after Kuruni had retired behind the mat. The day for the beggar family had ended.

I went to bed wondering what made this couple sustain this life. What might the husband be thinking when he has his last smoke, alone on the empty corner in front of the shop? Does he plan strategies to make more money without being caught, so that he can save enough money to rent a proper place for his family? He perhaps does not tell her how he was nearly beaten

---

[15] It is rolled in a bay leaf, rather than paper.

up by ruffians because he was in the wrong neighborhood. It is a precarious profession, I thought, with very little income or security, and a lot of hazards.

Where on earth, I wondered, does the couple sleep? My aunt told me that on nights in the summer months, when everything had quieted down, they rolled out a burlap bed right on the sidewalk—they found their privacy in the wide open world. I thought that on cold nights it must be strangely cozy for them to cuddle together with the whole family in the tiny space, separated from the world by the tattered mat.

As I became more fascinated by Kuruni's family I looked for an opportunity to make closer contact. I wanted to talk to them directly. So far, I was only observing from a distance—or hearing another's observations.

One morning, an unexpected opportunity arrived. Kuruni's little girl came and stood below our balcony to beg for a piece of bread from the maid, who was hanging the wash. This was unusual. For some reason, Kuruni never made her rounds in the immediate neighborhood. When I heard the voice of the maid admonishing the girl, I went out on the balcony and asked the child to come upstairs. I then gave her some food, and she told me that her mother was sick.

"Look," I said, giving her still more food, "if your mother needs anything, you come straight to me. Don't be afraid." I raised my voice so the maid would hear what I was saying. She was making disapproving signals to me, as if to say, "Is it a good idea to indulge these people?"

A few days passed. Kuruni's daughter did not come back. I wondered about Kuruni's condition and kept an eye open for anything unusual happening near the shop. I was also thinking of how I might use the material for a brief paper in anthropology. I could title it "Culture of Poverty: An Example of Survival," or something similar. I went to the balcony early one morning to see what the weather was like. The beggar family was back in its old routine.

Kuruni was on her feet. To my surprise, she looked up and smiled at me. I craned my neck and called to her to come up that afternoon if she had time. I did this on an impulse, perhaps because she herself had acknowledged my existence first. It was very unusual to invite beggars to a middle-class home. They came to the doorstep to beg, not to be invited in. I did not think Kuruni would really come. I had chosen the afternoon because that was the only time I could expect to be alone in the house. The intrusive maid would be gone and my aunt would be taking her nap.

Kuruni came to the open door but did not knock. She looked quite at ease as she stood waiting to be asked in. I took her to the terrace, where it was most private.

"I heard you were sick," I said. "Are you quite well now? Why didn't you send your daughter for some more—?" I could not finish my sentence. The woman did not appear in need of my mercy.

"Oh, that was nothing," she said. "I get a little fever once in a while. If I rest a day or two I'm on my feet again. With my family, I do not have the luxury of getting really sick." She smiled slightly and looked at me directly. "I haven't sent my daughter again because, you see, I never know how she will be treated. But you were kind to her. Do you think you can spare some old clothes? Not for me, for my mother-in-law. She finds it hard to keep warm at night."

"I'm sure I can find some," I responded. "Come back the day after tomorrow at this time. I shall sort some out.... Tell me, how do you manage to hold your family together? I have been watching you all from the balcony. I really admire your..." Again I could not say what I wanted to say. Words seemed inadequate.

"I don't know what you mean," she said, with a look of curiosity. "We are quite happy, actually. We have a place to sleep and my husband is healthy and earns good money. I have nothing to complain about." She spoke confidently. "And I can still keep my children with me. They don't have to be crippled to become beggars. I know we beg and depend on the kindness of people like yourself. But I am fortunate to have my whole family with me. What about you? Do you have children?"

"No. I don't have any children," I answered, noticing how discreetly she avoided the word *husband*, "although I was married once. Now I live alone and work. I suppose you are more fortunate than many. I see how you treat your mother-in-law with respect and affection."

"Oh well, that's nothing. She is a good woman, no trouble at all. She looked after my children when they were young and we had nowhere to live. We moved from place to place. Those were hard times."

"Don't you worry about your husband?" I asked. "He can be caught, beaten, even arrested." I felt ashamed of my direct question as soon as it was asked.

"So you've heard," she returned, softly. "Yes, I do worry when he is late coming home. So far, Mother Kali[16] has been kind to me. I know if I live a good life she won't let anyone hurt him...."

"Do you know what time it is?" she enquired. "I should be going. I must give my mother-in-law her tea. I shall come the day after tomorrow, then. Or, if you like, you could just make up a bundle and drop it from the balcony."

"No, no," I said. "I don't want to do that. I want to see you again and talk a bit more." I was embarrassed that I was not more hospitable to this woman who seemed to need so little, poor as she was. Should I have offered her tea? No one offers beggars tea; only food, and then only when they beg.

I couldn't get Kuruni out of my mind. The bright vermilion on her unwashed hair-parting announced that she was a married woman. But that did not seem to make her who she was. She was a woman with her own dignity: her ragged and dirty sari, her cracked heels and chipped fingernails—nothing could spoil that.

When she came again, to pick up the old clothes, I was no longer embarrassed. I felt honored to be able to help her. *One is blessed when one gives alms.* For the first time I understood the meaning of this Buddhist saying.

* * *

I returned to Calcutta six months later, after my work in the villages was done, and went to see my aunt. When I stepped out onto the balcony, I noticed a change in the space below the little shop. It was now used as storage for packing-containers. My aunt told me that the police had come a month before and taken

---

[16] Kali is the fierce Hindu goddess—she also has a healing and protective aspect.

away Kuruni and her family. No one knew where or why. Perhaps no one really cared.

Although I was worried about her husband, I knew Kuruni herself would adjust, no matter what. Though the family had disappeared into the vast crowds of the city, I knew that Kuruni would make a home for them somewhere. But the little shop at the street corner—and the wide Lansdowne Road—had lost something remarkable.

— *1966–1967* —

Fertile Sand

I went to the villages of West Bengal early in 1967, and was soon able to identify aspects of the culture that required particular study.

How often are lower-caste families invited to the homes of their upper-class counterparts? What kind of exchanges take place between castes on various ritual occasions? These are the sort of questions I raised in my research. There were questions, as well, about which I was more curious. For example: How do families of a given caste find husbands for their daughters, girls who grow faster than the vines of the newly-planted green squash after the rains?

I was often struck by the likeness of the smooth skin of the growing vines to that of the pubescent girls. They both seemed to have a fresh glow that commanded my attention far more than did the clean, white pages of my American-made notebook. But then, I had also seen the vines wither as they lay upon the dry earth not long after the autumn harvests.

In a market one morning I broke from my concentration on social customs when I sensed the undeniable profusion of *color* around me—the green of the melons and the yellow of the pumpkins, the red and orange of the peppers—all so full and fresh. It was glorious.

"Where do these melons and pumpkins come from?" I asked a woman at one stall. She told me they were from the *charas,* the narrow islands of sand in the drying beds of the receding rivers.

The *charas* are very fertile. There grow the best and the biggest of melons, cucumbers, and pumpkins. They lie all over the sand, which is so flat and low that from a distance it looks as if the fruit and squash were floating on the near-empty rivers. No one can steal it because it is so big. In four months of heavy growth, these vines make up for the rest of the year. Later, when the rains come to give birth to the rivers again, the *charas* disappear.

I have seen these rivers in the dry winter months, in the monsoon season, and in autumn. It's hard to believe the difference. At first, a river is only a broad swath of sand with a trickle of water at its middle. Next, it is a seething current of water and mud, amazing in its power. Then, it fades to pools and threads of shallow or stagnant water interspersed with fertile islands of sand, the *charas*.

I decided to go to the river and see a *chara* for myself. I left the market and reached the banks within minutes, then crossed a shallow creek, all that was left of the still-receding river. I had to lift my sari up to my knees to avoid getting it wet in the muddy water. I was not sure why I had to go. Was I interested in the size and quantity of the produce, or in something else? Perhaps I wanted to touch it, as if by touching the smooth skin of a melon I could take on the magic of its color.

"Even a 'dying' river is fertile in this country," I said to myself as I gained the edge of a *chara*. It was then that I heard a gasping, bleating cry.

For a moment I mistook the prolonged yet broken wail for a human cry. Then, suddenly, it was clear that an animal was in pain. It sounded like the recurring cries of a cat or a sick dog at night in the alleys of Calcutta. The sand gave way to a tangled hedge of hibiscus bushes, separating me from a small grassy clearing. The wail came from the clearing. I could see a hut not too far beyond. I thought it odd for a hut to be there, at the center of this island of sand and low-lying vegetation. When I climbed over the hibiscus bushes I saw a goat—on its back with its front legs pointing toward the sky and its hind ones almost hidden behind a very big belly. Sand coated its black hide. When, with a loud cry, it rolled over on its side, I realized that it was in labor.

I came forward. Her shoulders and spine were bent with pain. I did not dare look at her eyes, nor at the rictus of her muzzle. I was afraid I would see a woman's face. Her cry pierced my skin like a sharp instrument. I looked to see if anyone else were around. Someone from the village, who knew about such things, was needed here. I was shaken from my torpor by another screeching bleat: she had begun to give birth. I covered my ears and eyes for a moment and then ran for the hut.

Standing at the door, I heard the groan of a human being, unmistakable this time. I looked inside, where I saw a woman lying on a palm-leaf mat with a dirty quilt covering her legs. She was groaning rather softly, but stopped from time to time. She turned her thin face from the pillow to see who had come. She showed little surprise or alarm, only suppressed pain. I mumbled something about the goat and asked if there were anyone other than herself who could help with the situation outside. Her face lit up instantly; she tried to get up, but she could not raise her body. I saw then that she, too, was in labor. The happy expression on her face faded and she let out a cry, her head dropping onto the dirty pillow.

"Oh, my Bichuli is having her kid and I cannot be there to help," she uttered rapidly. "Whoever you are, oh woman from the town, be kind to us. Do go and help her, please." She gasped. "I cannot move. I think it's time for me, too. My poor Bichuli."

The woman's face contorted in a tremor of pain and she began turning from side to side. She clutched the bamboo post behind her pillow. I stood there watching her large abdomen as she moved one way, then the other, again and again. A brass water jar next to the woman's mat was now rolling and spilling its contents on the dirt floor. It had been knocked over by her flailing arm.

She had long black glossy hair that had loosened from its braid. She did not have a vermilion mark either on her forehead or in the parting of her hair; therefore she was not a married Hindu. Her sari-border was red, however. She had long brass earrings but no nose-ring or bangles; she was not a married Moslem. She was pregnant and alone.

The realization that there was no one in the hut to help her or her goat sent a chill though my spine. I became very frightened. Outside, the goat was quiet now. The woman herself had also become silent. But I could not move. The dimly-lit hut, with its bamboo walls and dirt floor, held me captive. I was keenly aware of the musty smell of the woman's hair-oil. I remained petrified until the woman gave out another cry.

"Please, good lady," she implored between her gasps. "Go and see if my goat is all right. On the south side of the yard you will find a hearth with a big clay pot over it. Go quickly and make a fire. Use some of the paddy-husk. You must draw water from the well on the other side of the hut and boil it in the pot. You must help Bichuli to give birth. The afterbirth can be buried under the big banana tree." She stopped to catch her breath, pointing toward the yard with a trembling finger, when another contraction took hold of her whole body. She screamed louder than before.

For a moment the world around me evaporated and I was whirled amid a spiral of different objects: the goat, the woman, the dirty pillow, the brass water jar. In another circle spun the pumpkins, the melons, the sticky sand and the muddy creek.

"Go quickly, please," came her voice. For the first time since I had entered the hut, I moved. The whirling disappeared and I stopped feeling. I simply acted.

I did all she had instructed me to do about the water. Then I moved toward the goat, who now lay very still. Her belly, shrunken, shook a little. By her side lay a small bundle that, also, was very still. I tried to move it. It was without life. I wondered if the goat knew her kid was dead. I wanted to throw up.

I managed to get back to the hut and told the woman that her goat and the kid were alive and well. She looked relieved. "Whoever you are, you are her mother," she said, closing her eyes. "You saved her life and her baby's. You are a godsend." She turned toward the wall and seemed to doze off.

I watched the woman, lying on her oily pillow all alone and waiting the birth of her child. My fear of a few minutes before now turned into exasperation. I became irritated with everything, including the woman's god who had sent me there to help them. I was trapped. I seemed to have lost any strength to think, to plan a course of action. Everything was quiet. The faint sound of snoring came from the woman. I was alone. I never knew such loneliness before: as if I found myself in a desert. I wanted to get away as far as I could.

I began to run, tearing through the hibiscus bushes at the edge of the clearing. I slogged across the sand of the riverbed and jumped over the muddy trickle that separated the island from the village. I took a rickshaw through the market to the busstand at the other end of the village. I took the bus to the railway station to catch the electric train. I got off at Howrah Station, and stood in the queue for a taxi. I stretched out on the back seat while the taxi drove for half an hour through the familiar sights, smells, and noises of Calcutta. I got out in front of my parents' house, paid the driver, and collapsed on a chair in the living room.

All this passed through my mind in seconds. And I did move at last. In my haste, I knocked the brass water jar with my toe. It rolled to the bamboo post and made a loud noise. The woman woke from her stupor and began to groan again. I went out, not waiting to hear if she was talking to me. When I reached the hibiscus hedge, near which lay the pumpkins and melons, I did not stop to see if the goat was still alive.

I ran through the leaves and vines of melons and pumpkins. My slippers got tangled. My sari got caught on the rough burrs of the empty vines, left when the squash was picked. Nor did I see any yellow pumpkins anywhere. Had someone picked them all?

I returned with the village midwife an hour later, after I had gulped down a cup of hot tea in a shop. I brought a jar of milk. We heard the cry of a newborn baby from the other side of the creek. I looked at the midwife, who smiled with relief. I pointed out the hut to her, and gave her some money and the jar of milk. I asked her to do all she could to take care of the mother and the child. I did not mention the goat. A chilling thought ran through my mind. Had the woman survived the birth?

When I returned to the village, I passed through the market again. I saw the baskets of melons and pumpkins. The melons looked pale and the pumpkins looked dry. The soft green and the smooth yellow were gone.

— 1967 —

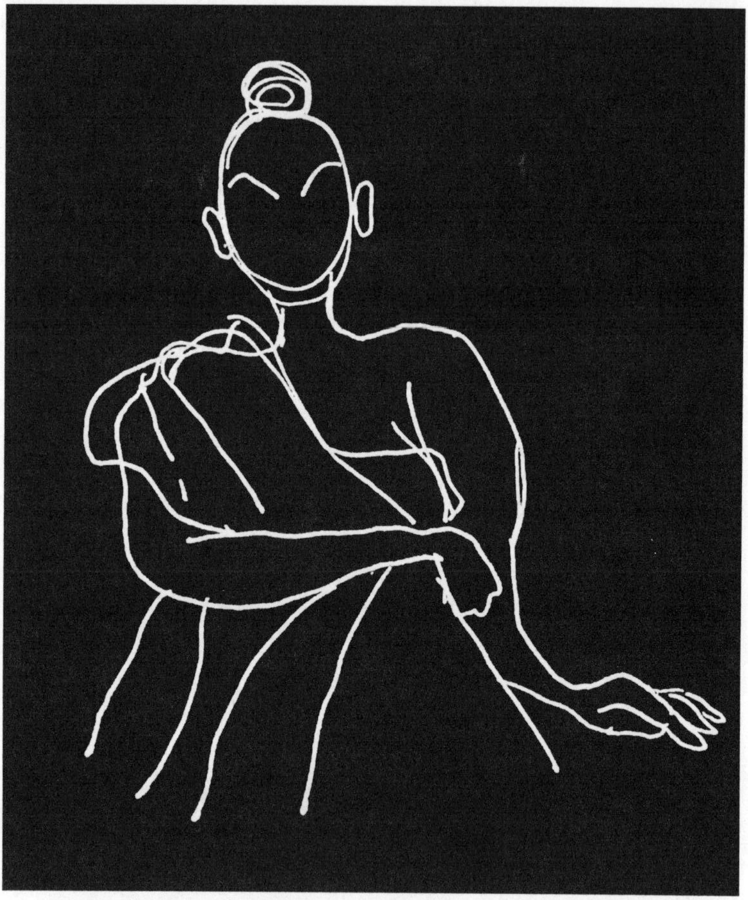

A Marigold

One very bright morning in May, while at my lodgings in Bishpara, a village in West Bengal, I was overtaken by a strange mood. I lingered under the tamarind tree in the yard, where I had eaten my breakfast an hour earlier. Everything around me felt oppressive.

I let my body take the shape of the dilapidated cane chair in which I sat, and watched the flies gather along the rim of the enamel cup on the table. The tea was still in it. A fly slipped into the cup and drowned in the lukewarm liquid. A weak little wind came from nowhere, causing a few dead leaves to drop from the tamarind. These fell on my hair, my shoulders, and my lap. The leaves looked ugly. Why, I thought, doesn't the wind send me a sprig of fresh green leaves?

The sun was scorching, although it was only eight in the morning. I had been debating whether I should attempt my usual tour through the streets "to observe the people in their natural habitat." But I felt tired and lazy. I could not even bring myself to leave the chair to see if someone would draw water from the well under the jackfruit tree so that I could have a cold rinse.

I could not move. The buzz of the flies and the vague murmur of the wind through the tamarind branches lulled me further and further toward lethargy. I stayed there and felt more oppressed.

I tried to adjust to my surroundings, to look beyond the flies, the dead leaves, the snapped and sagging chair. The Bengali newspaper of the previous day lay at my feet. I saw the headlines on the outspread page; the black amorphous print did not make any sense. The small square in the upper right hand corner, which usually held an advertisement for a fabulous writing ink or some equally fabulous painkiller, did not seem to be there. I felt dazed.

My thoughts drifted to the work I was doing there in the village. To what, I wondered, will all these "studies" amount?

What am I trying to find? Whatever conclusions I draw from all these careful observations will not add a whit to anything. What good is it to tell a handful of people that the village called Bishpara has twenty sub-castes which exchange gifts on the first full moon after the spring equinox, or that the age of circumcision among the Moslem boys of the village ranges between nine and twelve? The flies will not stop gathering along the rim of the teacup at these revelations, nor will the wind stop causing the leaves to drop.

I was not at all keen on going out for my usual tour. I will linger under the tamarind tree instead, I thought, and burn my skin in the rising heat. It felt intolerable but real, and I lingered. I was up for nothing.

Nonetheless, I *had* to move. My surroundings—the flies, the leaves, the chair beneath me—all began to appear gross. An unbroken ring of flies now spanned the rim of the cup. The sight turned my stomach. I wondered, Does anyone in this world not loathe flies? The heat was producing beads of perspiration along my forehead, neck, and spine. I could taste the sticky salt as it trickled down my face. I felt ugly and loathsome. The early morning breeze now stopped completely, yet the brown dead leaves kept dropping on me.

I got up. I went inside, picked up my sunglasses and umbrella, and stepped out into the street. I had to get out before Mr. Das, my assistant, arrived. Yes, even the prospect of seeing Ketan Das, all bathed, groomed, and enthusiastic for work, seemed depressing. In the past, Mr. Das, a man barely five feet in height, with neatly combed, oily hair, who always carried a torn plastic briefcase and a broken umbrella, would manage to lift my mood. I found his very appearance and his endless stories about the two American anthropologists, his previous employers, quite funny. Right now I was apprehensive about his enthusiasm and his chatter. I did not wish to be pushed into any action by anyone.

I stepped into the street and began to walk, without any plan or direction in mind. After an hour of careless meandering, I realized that I was walking toward the river. Perhaps I wanted to plunge in and cool off, and wash away the dirt, the perspiration, and the whole feeling that had depressed and paralyzed me.

But before I got to the river, which I could now see, I came upon a cluster of tin-roofed huts, all huddled together. Beyond this point lay a span of riverbank full of weeds and mounds of clotted clay. To reach the river I would need to pass through this settlement or go around another quarter of a mile.

I had never noticed these huts before. They were obviously outside of the village boundary, like those of gypsies on the edge of a European town. I wondered if the huts were indeed those of gypsies. As I became more curious, my wish to reach the river dissipated. I moved toward the row of tin roofs. I had already begun to feel better.

The first hut I came to had a small, cleared patch of garden at the front, where bushes of red-spotted marigolds were in full bloom. I told myself that only a flower as sturdy as the marigold can bloom in such weather. But there was a vine of jasmine too, climbing up the south side of the hut, and a *tulsi* plant[17] at a corner of the little yard. A couple of gardenias were opposite the tulsi, but had no blossoms; their sleek green buds had yet to burst. I was impressed and pleasantly surprised to come upon this Garden of Eden so suddenly. Few villagers had such gardens, as a rule, because the wildflowers in this area grow so abundantly.

Yet here, in this garden, a tiny bush of white *bel*[18] grew as if it were tended with special care. The leaves were clean and shiny. The flowers looked very full and healthy. The soft, milk-white blossoms brought to mind the sight of new teeth in a child's mouth. As I bent down to smell the flowers, I could not resist letting my hot cheeks be caressed by the soft, cool blossoms. They must have been watered that morning.

"Who are you?" came a sharp voice. It was a shock. I felt as if I were transported to that other garden where a wayworn merchant was about to pluck a rose for his daughter and a beast emerged from behind the bush with a thunderous threatening roar. I stood up quickly and saw, at the door of the hut, only a young woman. She was looking at me with much disdain, while I looked back at her with embarrassment. Attempting a civil tone, I told her that I had been attracted by her beautiful flowers and that I had merely wanted to touch and smell them.

---

[17] *Tulsi* is a variety of tropical basil, considered a holy plant by the Hindus.

[18] *Bel* is a white fragrant flower that blooms in summer.

She looked at me shrewdly. "Never heard of anyone touching a flower in another's garden," she said, in a rather harsh dialect. "You must be from the city. Only a city woman would talk like that. You have to be from another place, otherwise you wouldn't dare to come here." She paused and smiled sardonically. "Have you lost your way? Are you alone? Where do you want to go? Take this road and walk straight ahead till you find a tea shop. Someone there will direct you." I was still recovering from the shock and confusion of the encounter.

"God! Are you deaf and dumb?" she continued. "Look, the way she is staring at me. Sorry I am in your way. To 'touch' the flowers, indeed. *How sissy!*" She uttered the last two words with a sneer and a lift of her nose.

Her words came so fast that I had no chance to say that I was not really lost and thought there was nothing "sissy" about touching a flower. My mood, which had changed a few minutes before, began to change again, this time for the worse. I felt like an intruder. This confrontation was so unexpected. During my five months' stay in the village, I had never encountered anyone so openly hostile.

I did not know what to do. Nevertheless, there was a sense of mystery about her that I could not ignore. It was hard simply to leave.

"Well, my dear lady of the city," she said, softer now, "hasn't anyone ever told you not to come this way? You look so innocent. I may even believe it if you tell me that a cloud picked you up from Calcutta and just dropped you right here." She shook with laughter.

I was put more at ease by this, but could not see why I should be warned by the villagers not to come. It is not a leper colony, I thought, is it? Then everything became clear. I now had a good look at her. Why, of course! *She is a prostitute.* The odd row of huts set away from the village, her surprise at my sudden appearance, her way of talking, her jewelry, clothes, and gestures all told me that she must be "one of them," as a villager might say. I was relieved at the discovery. I now understood her hostility, and I was determined to be friendly.

I must admit that my interest in her leapt to such heights not because she had such a beautiful garden but because I had always wanted to meet and "interview" a prostitute. I must not let this opportunity pass, I thought. No villager, including my assistant, would ever have directed me to this spot. I felt fortunate to have come upon this made-to-order situation in which I would be the first city-bred female anthropologist in India to interview a real prostitute right in her own house. I began to formulate a number of questions "to elicit information." I summoned all my tact for this delicate maneuver. The woman must have been watching my expression change. She looked a bit puzzled when I came toward her.

"What is the matter?" she asked. "Oh, now I know. You are looking for the one your husband comes to. I should have known. But the wives usually don't drop in like this. Anyway, I do not keep a ledger of my clients, nor does anyone else here, I assure you."

"Why bring yourself to this?" she sympathized. "Go home, and stop being too nice. Maybe then your husband will spend more nights at home. Now get moving, go! I have things to do." She made another sardonic smile. I did not move, but instead raised my right wrist to show her that I did not have a conch shell bangle; therefore, no husband.

"I shall tell you how I got here," I said. "But could I have a glass of water, please? I'm so thirsty from walking in the sun."

"What? You want a drink of water? Here?" She looked shocked and a bit suspicious.

I nodded and sat down on the steps of her hut. She stood silent for a moment, then suddenly smiled very openly and gently. Her face reminded me of a marigold: sturdy and bright, yet soft.

"How about some fresh lime juice in your water?" Without waiting for my reply, she went inside.

I mused over the magic of the situation that, after the initial difficulties, was bringing us together. The heat of the morning, my doubts and frustrations, the walk to the riverbank—all seemed so distant already. The atmosphere—and my mood—had changed. I began to relax. Now was the time to ask all my carefully chosen questions.

She came out with a ceramic glass of cool water with slices of lime floating on the top. I drank the water, then held the moist glass between my palms.

"You really do like to touch things, don't you?" she said, smiling softly again. "But why are you here? Are you writing stories about us?" Her expression had changed to a mischievous one. She was trying to place me. If I were not a wife, I must be a reporter. Why else would I visit her? I shook my head.

"You see," I said, "I had been trying to get some fresh air and so I walked toward the river. When I saw your beautiful garden I had to stop. It's your garden that has brought me here, and I really did not care to know who you might be." I suppressed the truth, that I had stayed when I had found out who she was. She looked half-convinced and made a little shrug of her sari.

Now it was harder for me to stay. I had no real excuse. I almost regretted that I had lied and had not told her that I indeed wanted to know her because of who she was. Perhaps she would have been happy to tell me all about her life. Perhaps she would have liked the idea of being in a story—in a book, the kind read by the wives of the men who visit her. Perhaps I had been stupid not to tell her the truth. As an anthropologist, I was at odds with myself.

"Do you intend to stay outside in the garden?" she asked with a yawn. "Or would you like to come in?" She seemed unconcerned, now that I had been "honest." It was not her headache anymore if I wished to enter her forbidden world. I believe I had flattered her by my interest in her garden. She had decided to tolerate this strange intruder.

I looked up to see if she was watching me. She was gone. I heard the rattling of pots and pans. Was she preparing to cook her noon meal? I took a chance and entered the hut. I found her in the kitchen, cutting up some vegetables with a knife. In front of her sat an enamel bowl of water, into which she dropped finely-chopped potatoes. I put my glass on the floor and sat down next to it. She looked at me.

"Don't you know anyone in the village? You must be very lonely. Poor city people. Do you study or work in an office? Why aren't you married yet? How old are you?" She asked all these questions spontaneously. I was delighted to make conversation and stay a bit longer. When I gave honest responses to all her queries, she looked pleasantly surprised. She washed her hands and wiped them in her sari, set the knife down, and began to ask more questions.

What followed was an interview in which *I* did the talking in reply to *her* questions. To my amazement, she knew all about my life by the end of an hour. "How fascinating!" she said. "Tell me more about yourself. Why don't you stay and eat with me? Would you like to?"

By then, however, I was a bit annoyed with myself for talking as much as I had—for my gullibility toward a prostitute who had made me talk about my life—and all of it the truth, too. I began to feel cheated. The beautiful garden, the cool drink, all were full of some kind of magic power that had trapped me and forced me to reverse my role. How uncanny, I thought.

"No, I do not have time to stay," I said, standing up and shaking my head vehemently. "Already I have wasted a lot of time." I now recalled all the warnings I had heard about the diseases with which prostitutes are associated. Strange that I could forget.

"It must be quite late," I added. I had forgotten my watch in the throes of my mood that morning. "I ought to be going."

"Please come back when you take a walk to the river again," she said, disappointed. "We shall talk. I never met anyone like you. No one talks to us the way you do. You took me to your world. I never lived among your kind of people.... You see, my grandmother came to this line, and here I am." Then she looked into my eyes.

"You knew from the beginning, didn't you? I am sorry I was so nasty. It's hard to trust people who hate us. Please do not mind. I feel good now that we talked. Do come back, but come only around this time of day. How long will you be in the village? Will you tell me more about your work, your travels and your friends? I want to know it all." I hurried out of the hut. She followed me to the door. It had begun to feel hot again.

"I shall try to come back," I said, walking through the garden, "if I can avoid the eyes of the villagers. After all, they may not like the idea that I have talked with a *prostitute.*" I uttered the last word a bit louder than the rest. The spotted marigolds were still very bright. The bel blossoms still looked soft and fragrant. I did not pause to touch them. I was in a hurry to leave.

When I had gotten out of her yard, I stopped to regain my composure. I saw an old couple sitting in front of the next hut. They looked ancient. I was struck by the whiteness of the woman's black-bordered sari, and by the silver-grey hair of the man. I turned to have a closer look. The woman was trying to clip the toe-nails of the man, but her fingers shook too much. This amused the man. He began to laugh, and then they laughed together. Their faces were furrowed with laughter and their eyes nearly closed from it. I had a strong desire to touch their faces.

Walking back to the village, I felt the noon heat a thousand times worse than before, but I was distracted. I was thinking about the young prostitute, how skillfully she won me over. Strangely, my surprise was mixed with pleasure. I then thought of the old prostitute, how she cared for the old man and laughed with him. My surprise now mixed with sadness. I knew I would not return to visit the prostitute whose name I had not bothered to ask.

I did, however, look in the market for marigolds. There were none. Perhaps, they flourished only in small gardens at the very edge of a village.

— *1967* —

Nearly two decades later, while traveling, I felt the familiar urge to record my experiences. Doing so brought back memories of earlier unexpected encounters. These two decades were spent in finishing my doctorate in anthropology, in teaching, both in Denver, Colorado and in Zurich, Switzerland, and in studies—and intensive personal analysis—in Jungian psychology. During this period I visited my family in India several times. The following two stories, chronologically the last in this book, took place in such travels back to the Indian subcontinent. Despite the change in time and place, my surprise and delight in human nature continued unabated.

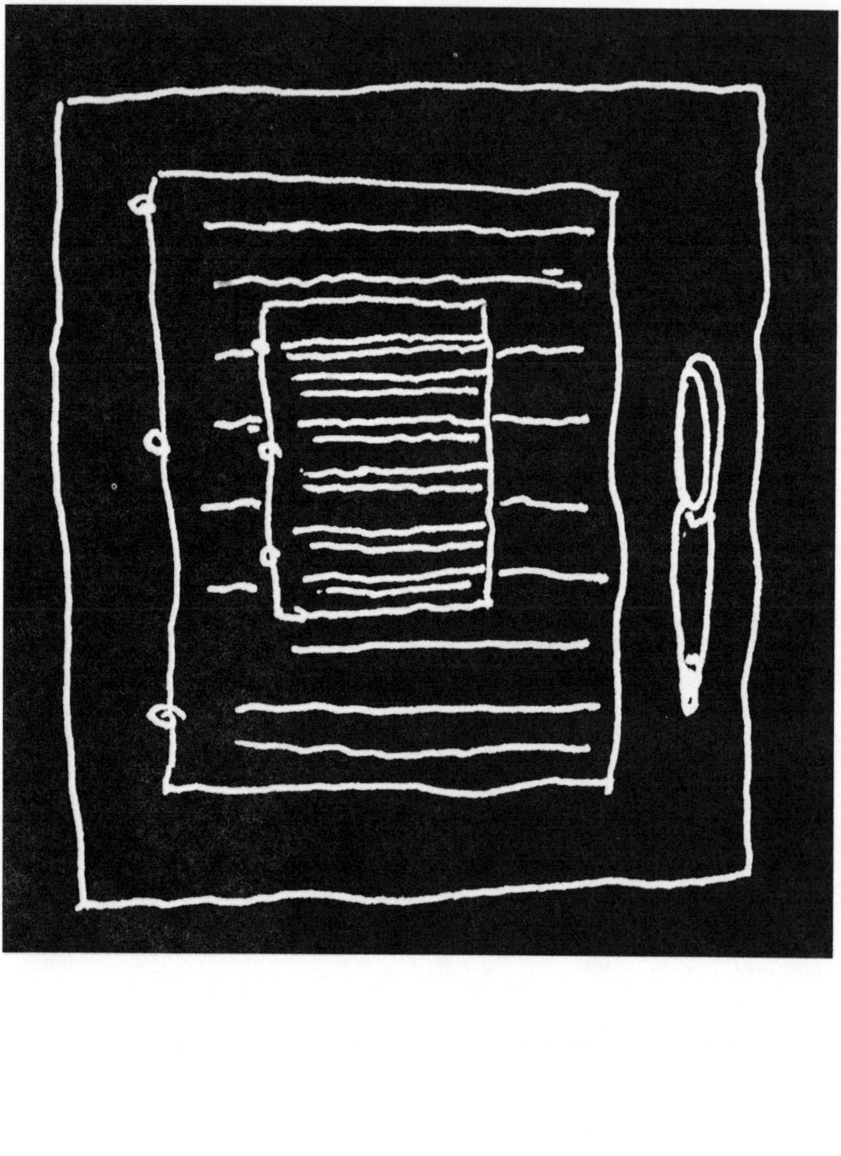

HOSPITABLE STRANGERS

The plane began to move across the tarmac of Calcutta airport. "Is this your first trip to Dhaka?"[19] asked my neighbor, a European man, as we buckled our seatbelts.

"Yes," I answered. "Both sides of my family come from Bangladesh[20] originally, but I have never been there myself."

A flight attendant welcomed the passengers aboard in Bengali through a microphone and added the usual details about the safety measures.

"My name is Werner Brendt," said my neighbor when the attendant had finished. From the name it was clear he was German. I told him mine.

"I presume you are Hindu," he said. "Isn't your religion full of gods and goddesses, whereas Islam has none?"

"Yes...?"

"I am also curious..." he said. "How does your family feel being uprooted from their ancestral land? There must be a lot of animosity."

"In 1947, when the partition took place, they were upset, of course," I said. "Fortunately, most of my family were already living in India. They lost a lot of property but escaped the worst riots. Now, after nearly four decades, the pain and anger are nearly gone. Hindus who are well-off today don't resent the move as much anymore. But something similar happened in your part of the world—in your own country."

"Right, right," he said, as if to dismiss my remark. "But I'm not clear about how the two religions lived together so long before the partition." He seemed now to be addressing himself. Perhaps he was aware of asking too many questions.

---

[19] The capital city of Bangladesh. (Once spelled Dacca.)
[20] Once India's East Bengal, this area became the eastern part of Pakistan and, in 1971, the independent republic of Bangladesh.

"You see," I said, "until the politicians got involved, the situation was under control. The Bengali Moslems had shared the same culture for centuries with their Hindu neighbors, except in religious practices. There were occasional conflicts, but never too severe. Besides, the Hindus were mostly in control of the land and money..." I was interrupted by a flight attendant who came by with some candies.

"Please continue," Herr Brendt urged, once he had put a candy in his mouth.

"Well, in my view, the Bengali Moslems have had a much harder time since the partition because they shared very little with Pakistan besides the religion. You must know about the bitter battles they fought to gain independence. Since the birth of Bangladesh in the early seventies they have had additional battles to fight: poverty..." Before I could finish, the attendant came back with coffee, tea, and snacks. I was glad to be interrupted. I disliked being drawn into political discourse with a stranger. I did not want to lecture Herr Brendt on Bangladesh.

"What brings you to Dhaka?" I asked, before he could pose another question.

"I work for the World Bank," he answered. "I'm here to discuss the terms and conditions of a loan sought by the government of Bangladesh. I'm very aware of the plight of this land. Not only are they one of the poorest nations in the world, but, as you know, they are also faced with frequent natural disasters. But please, tell me, how is the relationship between the Bengalis of Bangladesh and India today?"

I began to wonder if he were writing a report on the human side of his work. Perhaps he needed data he could not gather in his official position. I became a bit more sympathetic. I had long experience of collecting information, no matter where and how. Meanwhile, the attendant returned with more tea and coffee.

"Right now," I said, after a sip of warm tea, "the situation seems to be stable, at least among the educated middle-class. As I said, because of our shared language, literature, and food, the Bengalis on both sides of the border have some deep connections—despite the religious difference. I myself have a few close friends in Bangladesh. In fact, I'm on my way to visit a Moslem friend in Dhaka now."

PEOPLE OF THE PLAINS

A routine greeting and message from the pilot stopped Herr Brendt from asking more questions. I opened a newspaper to show that I was not terribly interested in further dialogue on the topic. What I did not tell him was that, being away in America for most of the last two decades, I had experienced the political situation in South Asia by way of the press and media only—and thus might, quite possibly, be biased. I had little problem sharing the writings and songs of Tagore[21] and the delicacies of our common kitchen with my Bengali Moslem friends. I was looking forward to a few days in Dhaka doing exactly that.

When the short flight of just under an hour brought us to Dhaka, the airport looked unexpectedly empty for mid-afternoon. A row of uniformed guards stood between the plane and the terminal building. Once in customs, we were told the news: a twenty-four-hour nation-wide strike had been declared that morning.

The Bangladeshi passengers departed quickly. They must have made previous arrangements. Herr Brendt was met by a couple of foreigners who escorted him out to a Volkswagen bus with *World Bank* written on the side and driven by a liveried chauffeur. In less than ten minutes I found myself alone with my suitcase. The only other traveler was a reporter from Calcutta. Even he had not known about the strike before leaving. So it could not be that serious, I thought.

We managed to find a booking clerk and asked him about changing money. He seemed in a big hurry to close shop. It was from him that we learned for the first time that it was a total strike and the airport was virtually closed. We had better settle on the sofas in the lounge for the night, he said. No taxi or bus would go into the city until the next day, more than twelve hours away. He also informed us of a rumor that arson and riots had broken out in certain parts of the city as a result of clashes between the public and the army.

The news was not that disorienting for me. In my long experience of travel to different parts of the world, I had run into many unexpected situations, including canceled flights, near-crash

---

[21] Rabindranath Tagore (1861–1941) was a Bengali poet, writer, composer, and painter. Born in Calcutta, he visited East Bengal in the 1890's. He won the Nobel Prize for literature in 1913.

landings, and customs harassments due to unintended errors. Besides, I had the telephone number of my friend in Dhaka. All I needed was to call her and she would make some special arrangements. Her family was well-connected.

The reporter, in the meantime, was getting ready to camp, putting two sofas together and spreading his raincoat over them. He appeared well-practised in such things. I dragged my suitcase around the terminal, looking for a telephone. In a few minutes I saw a young woman who looked like an airport employee. In high heels, make-up, and a name-tag pinned to her nylon sari, she looked official and quick.

"Didn't you know about the strike?" she asked, in a friendly tone of voice. "When did you arrive? No other aircraft will be landing here in the next twenty-four hours. We're shutting down everything except the emergency departments." She looked then at my face, which must have shown some concern for the first time. "Please come with me to my office. You can use the phone there."

In her little office, which was obviously the public address center for the whole terminal, she made a few announcements about the cancellation of all flights. I was struck by her voice and accent over the loudspeaker, which were totally different from how she'd spoken to me. She then asked for the telephone number of my friend in Dhaka—and dialed it for me, handing me the receiver.

I asked for my friend and a young man replied, with no sign of recognition toward my name, that she had left for London three days before because of a family crisis. When I explained who I was, he said that she had tried to contact me in Calcutta by telegram and telephone, without success. I told him of my predicament, and he said he could do nothing until the strike was over.

"Tomorrow I could send my car if you can somehow remain at the airport. My driver will not agree to drive through the city today. I'm really sorry." He hung up after more apologies.

My annoyance with the telephone and telegraph systems of our countries was exacerbated by the tone of the young man. What did I expect him to do, anyway? I had to admit that I was in one of those situations when no target was available upon which to vent my frustration.

Overhearing my side of the conversation, the young woman in the office gathered what was happening. I think my face told much of the story.

"Didi," she said, without any hesitation, "I see you're in a fix. Why don't you come to my place for the night? It's within the airport compound. I am off in an hour. This way at least you'll have some rest tonight, though my house may not be suitable for you."

"Thank you so much," I said, quite surprised by her offer, "but I can't impose on you. You met me only a few minutes ago." As I spoke I had to consider whether I really had any other alternatives. I also could not help wondering about unexpected compensations in life.

"It's really no imposition," she said. "You will be like one of the family. I cannot leave you in this deserted airport all by yourself. Please."

"Thanks," I said. "I guess I have hardly any choice left. I will come with you." I sat down on the only other stool in the booth and relaxed for the first time since my arrival an hour before.

"I shall be ready as soon as my replacement comes," she said. She left the booth in quick steps and came back with a cup of tea and a samosa.[22] "Please have these and relax. I shall try to locate my regular rickshaw. I hope he hasn't disappeared because of the strike." She smiled and left. I had not considered that the employee quarters might be beyond walking distance. Obviously the employees were not provided with a shuttle bus or anything like that.

The rickshawala agreed to take both of us and the suitcase only after he was promised a heavy tip. Once in the rickshaw, with my suitcase at our feet, we introduced ourselves formally. Her name was Maya, which could be a name for either a Hindu or a Moslem. In Bengali it means 'compassion'. It suited her perfectly.

A brief trip in the bicycle-rickshaw took us to a row of apartment buildings stuck out in the middle of a large open field devoid of trees or landscaping. I wanted to pay the rickshawala myself, but Maya would not allow me. She pointed out that I had no local currency.

---

[22] A fried, triangular pastry stuffed with meat or vegetables.

We climbed four flights of concrete stairs to the top floor of her building. Children watched with curiosity from the box-shaped balconies of other apartments. It had not occurred to me that these might be family quarters. Assuming that Maya was single I was expecting some sort of a "single's pad"—the kind nurses and flight attendants usually occupy. But these looked like regular urban housing for lower-income families.

Outside the apartment door I could hear talking and the noise of children. Maya asked me to come in. Before I could make a move she had taken my suitcase and drawn aside the flimsy curtain on the doorway.

I stepped into a room almost wholly occupied by a large bed. It was covered with a colorful cotton spread, on one side of which was a healthy-looking baby, asleep under a small collapsible mosquito net. Two men were sitting on the bed, smoking and chatting. A middle-aged woman stood nearby, her sari covering her head and part of her face. They all looked up, seeing a stranger with Maya, who now also pulled her sari over her head in respect to the men.

"Didi is going to spend the night with us," she announced gently, in the Dhaka dialect. "She was stranded in the airport. In Calcutta they didn't even tell her about the strike." I could not help noticing the transformation in Maya's manners. She sounded subdued, though quite firm in her decision to invite me.

The younger of the two men moved nearer to the sleeping child, making room for me to sit on the bed. Maya introduced everyone: her husband, father-in-law, and sister-in-law. A group of children stormed in and out of the room, holding onto one another, imitating a train. The baby awoke at their hissing and whistling. Maya picked up the baby, kissed it, and gave it to the father-in-law. She asked if I would like to wash up.

We passed through two other rooms, again with beds covering most of the space, to a narrow hallway. Next to the bathroom was the kitchen, where an older woman with her head completely veiled was busy cooking. Maya introduced her mother-in-law to me.

Back in the first room, which was Maya's bedroom, I was then served tea and French toast. I remembered a box of sweets I had brought from Calcutta for my friend's family. I unpacked them and handed the box to Maya, my first and only token of gratitude for what she was doing for me. Her husband climbed down from the bed, saying that he had to get ready to leave for his night-shift at the airport. He wished me a good rest that night and asked if he could do anything at the airport about my situation. I saw later that I would occupy the space in the bed he had left vacant that night.

After the tea, I relaxed—with a household of strangers, in which everything became familiar in little time. I was amazed by their acceptance of me, a Hindu woman from another country, class, and society.

In the course of the evening I learned that the older couple had four sons, two of whom lived in the city and served in the army. The father-in-law, a handsome man in his seventies with a trim goatee, worked in the storage facility at the airport. Maya had been married only three years and the baby was her first child. Her sister-in-law had four. Her husband and brother-in-law worked in the security department of the airport. Because four of them worked there they had been allotted this apartment. Otherwise they would have had to wait another four to eight years. The three-bedroom apartment was just big enough for the whole family except for the two sons who lived in the army quarters at the far end of the city. The older women stayed home to take care of the children and to perform other household chores. The mother-in-law managed the kitchen. A perfect joint-family system, I thought.

At nine in the evening we all sat down for dinner on individual mats on the floor. While the mother-in-law offered me big pieces of fried *hilsa* fish[23] and spicy chicken curry, she kept lamenting that they were not prepared properly enough for a guest like me. I was impressed not only by their hospitality, but by their humble generosity, of a kind I had not known still existed in this world. They also commented on my lack of prejudice in sitting and eating with Moslems. They did not know many Hindus who would do that. I remembered the questions Herr Brendt had asked me that very afternoon. What would he say, I wondered, if he were to see me in this household right now?

---

[23] A Bengali delicacy; a variety of shad.

I had a hard time accepting their compliments. I thought these were misplaced, since religious prejudice was not part of my upbringing. Even if it were, how could I not ignore it when I needed shelter so badly? How on earth could I convince them that what they were doing for me was far more commendable than my apparent lack of prejudice? I was only being selfish.

"You see," I addressed the father-in-law, "when your daughter-in-law offered me shelter for the night, it was *I* who was impressed. She did not have to do it. I haven't done anything special. I merely accepted her generosity and your hospitality. I'm the one who is eternally grateful."

"You are so kind," the father-in-law insisted. "We have done nothing. This is the house of a poor family, not fit for your comfort." He raised himself from the mat and walked to the bathroom to wash his hand. I followed him. Waiting at the door of the bathroom, I thought of my family when I was a girl, and felt very much at home. It took but a few hours for Maya's family to accomplish this feat. I had a notion that this might be the only time in my life I would experience such trust and hospitality from a group of strangers.

In bed that night I watched Maya feed her half-asleep baby. "Didi," she said, when she wanted to go to the kitchen to warm the milk. "Do you think you can keep an eye on him? I shall be back in a minute." The baby cried as soon as his mother put him down. I picked him up and rocked him a bit. By the time Maya returned he was quiet again. She looked surprised but pleased.

"I forgot to ask you…" she said, as I handed the baby back to her. "Do you have children?"

"No," I replied.

"You seem to know how to handle them." She smiled at me and looked down at her son. "See, you have a new aunt, who lives in the big city of Calcutta. Someday you will go and visit her." The baby did not seem to hear anything. He was fast asleep, with the bottle still in his mouth. Maya and I chatted about my family back home. We whispered, as I did in bed with my sisters when we met after a long time. Soon I too felt sleepy.

In the morning I found myself alone in the bed. The rest of the household was already awake. When I rose and joined the others, Maya's brother-in-law asked me what kind of fish I would like for lunch. He was going to a special fish market to get the freshest fish available. I was deeply touched.

Fish for the Bengalis—Hindus and Moslems alike—is not only a favorite edible, but an important symbol. There is hardly a Bengali ritual in which fish is not an essential ingredient. For a wedding, large carp are decorated and sent to the family of the groom. No feast, religious or secular, is complete without one or several fish dishes. Even the gods in heaven seem to have a special liking for it.

I had a very interesting talk with the father-in-law over breakfast. He was proud to say that in India in the early sixties he had been one of the guards in the Nehru household, when Jawaharlal Nehru[24] was alive. He felt very fortunate to have served that illustrious family. He also told me how gracious a gentleman Mr. Nehru was. The old man had a catch in his throat as he reminisced about his connection to the most significant family in Indian life and politics in this century. It had broken his heart to hear the terrible news of the assassination of Nehru's daughter, Indira.[25]

"How could anyone do such a horrible thing?" he asked.

"You are more fortunate than me," I said. "I knew the Nehrus only from a distance, through the press." I saw that his talk about the Nehrus remained purely personal. We both refrained from any political comments. Politics was not what was important for either of us. If only more Moslem fathers-in-law had opportunities to talk with their Hindu guests over breakfast, I considered, perhaps no politician could interfere with people's lives. Then, perhaps, I was being too naive.

An hour later I could smell the mouth-watering aroma of freshly-frying fish. Maya's mother-in-law was preparing an early lunch for me because I wanted to catch the first possible flight back to Calcutta, now that the strike had ended. Maya had left

---

[24] Nehru (1889–1964) was the first prime minister of independent India—from 1947 until his death. He established parliamentary government in India and maintained a neutralist foreign policy. He was born a Kashmiri Brahmin and was the son of Motilal Nehru, a disciple of Mahatma Gandhi.

[25] Indira Gandhi was the only child of Jawaharlal Nehru. She was Prime Minister of India for four terms and was assassinated by a Sikh extremist in 1984.

early for work, promising to make a reservation for my return trip. She would send someone to get me when it was confirmed.

I thought again of Herr Brendt's questions. Would Maya and her family have behaved with hate and anger if they had met me under different circumstances, in a different time? Sitting there on the big bed, next to the elderly gentleman who was playing with his grandson, I knew these people would be the same, no matter where or when.

After a delicious lunch of fish curry, I was ready to take leave of the wonderful family. One of the children came running to tell me that a big car had come for me. My friend's daughter-in-law had come in the car to the airport, where Maya had told her how to find me. She persuaded me to postpone my return for two days.

My friend's family had a big, beautiful house in an exclusive neighborhood. During the two days I spent there, I was busy meeting important people, eating rich and elaborate meals, and being well entertained. But I missed the four-room apartment where the only furniture was large beds, and where the aroma of fresh-cooked fish permeated the atmosphere and noisy children ran in and out of the rooms pretending to be trains.

— *1984* —

On The Way To Pune

The bus driver slammed on the brakes hard. We—all fourteen of us—held fast to the seats to avoid being banged around. "What on earth...?" exclaimed my father.

There was a thud from under the seat in front of me, and water flooded my sandals. Someone leaned over and stood the rolling clay pitcher up again. It now looked empty. The pitcher had been sitting in a straw doughnut. It had carried our drinking water, which had been boiled and chilled.

I looked out and saw in the road in front of us a small herd of goats. "Hei, hei, hoosh, hoosh," shouted a boy of ten or eleven as he waved a switch this way and that at the goats to hurry them across the road. It was not an uncommon sight on the roads and highways of India. Goats, sheep, cattle or a whole caravan of bullock-carts may turn up at any time.

It was the dry season. We were traveling in a mini-bus from Hyderabad, a city in south-central India, to Pune[26], in the southwestern part, and then on to Goa[27], on the southwestern coast, a distance of over four hundred miles. We had hired the bus, the driver, and a mechanic for ten days. The idea was to travel leisurely, sightseeing during the day and stopping every evening at a different town. There were fourteen of us: father, brothers, sisters, wives, husbands, and children. We were celebrating my father's eightieth birthday. Our ages thus fell into eight different decades, all with corresponding views and ideas regarding such a trip.

My father was somewhat frail, but healthy. Being a veteran traveler, he was as enthusiastic about the trip as the rest of us.

---

[26] This is one of the cultural capitals of South India. It is known for its schools, libraries, and spiritual centers.
[27] A beautiful city on the west coast of India, once the capital of Portuguese India.

His gentleness and concern toward the family were great assets in the organization of such a large group of travelers. He sat next to my eldest brother on the first seat behind the driver and pointed out interesting things to his two teen-aged granddaughters, my sisters' children, who teased each other and joked all through the trip.

In order to run things smoothly we had delegated various decisions and duties to individual family members. For example, my eldest brother dictated when we were allowed to stop for urgent needs. A minimum of three members had to agree on such an urgency.

This particular stop was not planned. After the goats were safely across the road, the driver started the bus again. It moved a few inches and stopped. "What now?" exclaimed my brother-in-law from the back seat, which bounced the hardest. The driver climbed down from his seat and got out to inspect what animal might be in the way this time. He circumambulated the bus a couple of times, then talked to the mechanic, who by now was also outside. The two had a discussion in their dialect, which was audible but not understandable by any of us.

"Where shall we get water now?" said my sister-in-law, who was holding the empty water pitcher. "It's a dry country. No tea shop will give us that much water, even if we paid them. Besides, that water wouldn't be worth drinking. We have miles to go; it's getting hot."

"That is correct," responded her husband, my eldest brother, a bit impatiently. "But now, we have other pressing problems to solve. We need to get the bus moving."

"She is right," said my younger sister, and turned to my sister-in-law. "We'll need water sooner than later, the way the heat is rising. Are you sure there is none left in the pitcher?"

My brother, in the meantime, shifted his attention and craned his head out the window. "What's going on?" he asked the driver. The driver stepped up to the window and declared that he and the mechanic thought that one of the front tires was flat.

"What do you mean, you and the mechanic *think*? It's either flat or not flat." Grudgingly, my brother got up from his seat and got off the bus to inspect the tire. No one among us was mechanically astute enough to detect such a simple problem as a flat tire, although several of us knew how to drive. The mechanic went to

PEOPLE OF THE PLAINS

the back and began to remove an extra tire. My brother got into the bus again, brushing his palms together as if he'd just got dirty from handling something. He announced that we would have to stop here for as long as they needed to change the tire—so this would be a good time "to use the bushes," if anyone so needed.

There was no tea shop or gas station, only a few thorny shrubs and acacia trees along the roadside. The earth all around was dry and cracked. We could see a few thatched roofs in the distance.

"A couple of us will go and try to find some water," said my sister-in-law, putting the water pitcher aside and taking up a flask. This time her husband didn't object to her concern.

"Good idea," he said. "The way the heat is rising we'll all need a drink soon." He turned to Father. "How are you doing?"

"I'm fine. Don't worry about me," Father assured him. "See if the baby has enough to drink. I'll get out and sit in the shade for a while. Be careful, the rest of you, and take umbrellas with you if you go looking for water. The sun is strong."

I volunteered to accompany my sister-in-law in search of water. Taking two umbrellas to ward off the sun, and the flask for the water, we began our exploration.

A ten-minute hike over hard ground, through thorny shrubs, took us to the thatch huts. There were three of them, clustered together around a tiny but clean yard. A dog sleeping under a guava tree was the only sign of life in the area. The huts appeared deserted. We looked around for a pond or well or waterpipe. The first two seemed very unlikely. It did not look like a village, only a few huts in the middle of dry, cracked land, which, however, would be fit for cultivation when there were adequate rains.

"Hello, anybody there?" I shouted in Hindi. After three or four such attempts, the bamboo door of one of the huts opened and an old man emerged. He must have been working behind the hut. His hands were dirty. He had a cotton cloth wrapped around his head like a coiled snake, presumably to protect his head from the sun. His bare body was thin and dark and he walked with a slight stoop. I guessed his age to be above seventy. I thought of my father, who must be very thirsty by now. The old man looked at us with surprise in his eyes, and with curiosity, not suspicion.

"Sorry to bother you like this," my sister-in-law said in Hindi. "Could we get some drinking water anywhere around here? Do you know of a well or a water-pipe?" The man looked as if he understood nothing of what she said. He took his turban off, shaking his head to the left and right. He opened the cloth and wiped his forehead with it. It was getting very hot. With the end of my sari, I too wiped my forehead, and moving to the guava tree for shade, put down the flask.

"He obviously does not understand Hindi," I said.

"*Nilum, nilum...*" said my sister-in-law, repeating the Telegu[28] word for water, and made hand gestures to mimic drinking. The old man's face registered a flicker of recognition.

"My father-in-law, father, old, thirsty, needs nilum," my sister-in-law implored, in a mixture of Hindi, Telegu, and sign language. After a few minutes she gave up and looked at me in desperation.

The old man looked at both of us and in the direction of the road. I could not tell if he could see the bus. He wiped his forehead, face, and neck with the cloth once more before wrapping it around his head again. We watched. Everything was quiet. The dog got up and shook the dust from its back, and walked slowly toward the old man. It seemed to take him an eternity. I looked at my sister-in-law, wondering if we should not be going back. The old man watched the approaching dog, then looked at us again. He signaled us to follow him.

We went with him around a hut, where he walked another ten or fifteen steps and squatted down under a mango tree. He lifted a clay plate from the ground—and there it was—a clay pot, buried to the rim, holding water, clear still water, so still that it reflected the branches of the mango tree above it. There could not have been more than a gallon.

"That's all the drinking water we have," said the old man, in a language of gestures and broken Telegu. "For my family, three sons and their wives, all working in the field right now—and the animals. But you can take some for your father. Old man should have water."

He gestured for the flask and poured the precious water into it with a coconut-shell ladle. The dog licked up whatever drops were spilled, before they soaked into the thirsty soil. I felt as if I

---

[28] The language spoken in the Indian state of Andhra Pradesh.

could do the same. My sister-in-law closed the flask and the old man covered the pot with the clay plate again.

I took a ten-rupee bill from my wallet and gave it to him for his tremendous kindness—for sharing his only reserve of water in this dry land. He seemed very surprised and shook his head vigorously, which loosened his turban again. I insisted.

"No money for water," he said. "Water for your old father. No, no."

This time we understood him perfectly. His gestures and expression spoke louder than his words. Now it was our turn to be surprised. How could he refuse such a windfall? Ten rupees[29] were quite a bit of money for a poor man in this season, when everything dries up, including all the ponds and rivers. He must have walked miles to get this water from someone's well.

We were quiet as we walked back to the bus. My youngest brother came toward us, motioning for us to hurry. The bus was ready to leave.

In the bus, no one seemed that interested in our adventure, except the children, who wanted some water to drink. In the back seats, the men were involved in what seemed a heated discussion about where and when to stop for lunch. My sister was eager to tell me how she managed to buy two ripe papayas at a bargain price from a villager who happened to pass by the bus.

"Thank God we hired the mechanic with the driver," said my eldest brother. "He knew exactly how to change the tire. We could easily be stranded otherwise."

My sister-in-law and I looked at each other, saying nothing. The breeze blew through the open windows of the moving bus, taking away my fatigue. I closed my eyes and thought of the thin old man and his clay pot of water under the shade of the mango tree. His lean, dark image kept appearing to me, even when I opened my eyes to look at the rapidly passing objects on the roadside.

* * *

---

[29] In 1984, approximately two U.S. dollars.

"How did you ever find the water this morning?" said my father at dinner that evening, when we had stopped for the night at a hotel.

As my sister-in-law narrated the story, I wondered if any one of us would have given away such precious water to two strangers who could easily afford to buy water anywhere.

"Incredible," said my father. "What a wonderful birthday gift that man has given me. Thank you two for making the effort and discovering such a soul."

— 1985 —

The three stories in the following section take place in La Jolla, a university town in Southern California—a great distance from Assam and West Bengal. A series of events had made it necessary that I return to America to begin graduate studies again, though this time in a different school. The essence of one such event was that I could not use the data on the Khasis for my doctoral dissertation. My fieldwork in Assam had been done under the auspices of the Anthropological Survey of the Government of India, which declared in a ruling that the data was its property, solely. Secondly, because of my formal separation from my first husband, it had become extremely difficult to find a decent job in Calcutta. Frustrated, I applied for admission to a new university in the United States. I entered the San Diego branch of the University of California—in La Jolla—in 1969. My plan was to "study" the Californians themselves. At the time, it had not been the convention to study a local group; to my knowledge, no anthropologist—native or foreign—had attempted such research. In the process of that study I learned a great deal about the California subculture. And I discovered, once again, that detachment and objectivity are not necessarily the best tools for understanding strangers. The more I struggled to understand the Californians, the less I seemed to empathize with them. I had yet to find that poetic balance between the subject and the researcher.

The West Coast Crowd

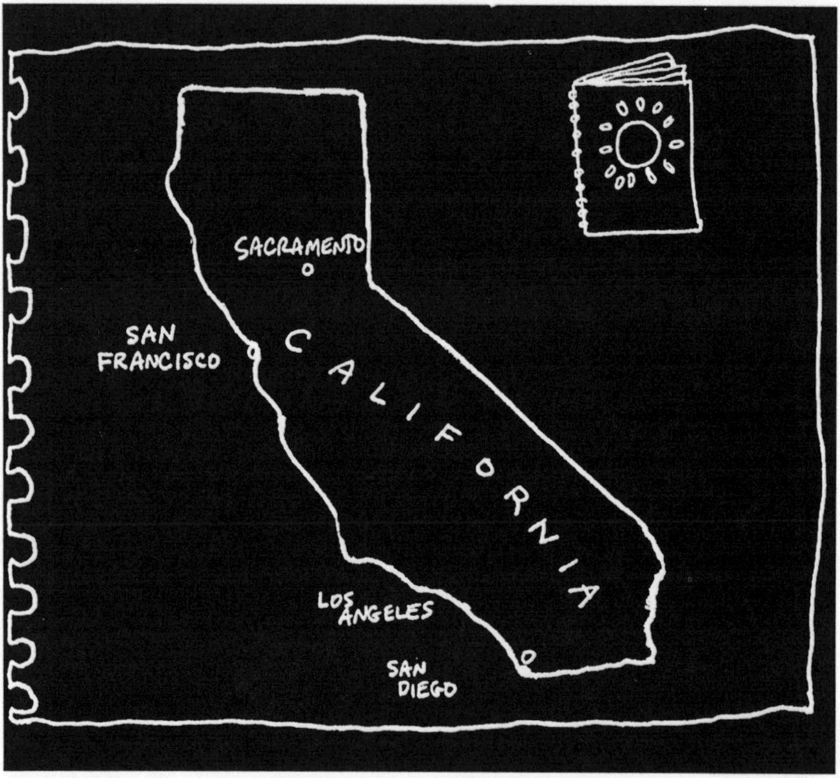
SACRAMENTO
SAN FRANCISCO
CALIFORNIA
LOS ANGELES
SAN DIEGO

Welcome to California

My fieldwork in India was over. After four years there, I was returning to America—to the southernmost campus of the University of California—for further studies. I had never lived in California before; I chose to now because, remembering the hard winters of the Midwest, I preferred a mild climate.

A letter from a woman named Joyce Wallace had reached me in India, inviting me to stay at her home in California for the two or three weeks before the start of classes:

This is a volunteer organization of stable families who open their doors and hearts to foreign students and help them adjust to the new environment. My family looks forward to providing you with a "home away from home." We'll help you move to wherever you wish—to the campus dormitory or to a private apartment. Please let me know the date and time of your arrival. I'll be at the airport to welcome you personally....

I was impressed by this gesture. The first time I went to America, no one had sent such a letter, no American family had so welcomed me. Of course, it had been the Northeast then, not friendly California.

As soon as I got my plane ticket, I wrote to Mrs. Wallace and accepted her hospitality. The day before I left, I spent the afternoon finding an appropriate gift for her. I chose a beautiful length of silk, embroidered with gold, ideal for making a dress or shawl.

When I arrived at the airport in California, I looked around for an eagerly waiting family or for a sign bearing my name. Since no one appeared, I went to the baggage claim. I had always thought it would be embarrassing to see my name in bold letters on a cardboard sign, held up above the heads of a crowd. Right now I wouldn't have minded at all. I was tired from the twenty-one-hour flight over a continent and an ocean. It would be good to go somewhere and rest.

I wheeled a luggage cart toward one of the exits and spotted a telephone booth. Nearly twenty minutes had passed since I landed. Perhaps Mrs. Wallace had forgotten. As I looked in my handbag for the telephone number, I saw an attractive woman in her thirties walking toward me, dragging a little girl. She kept brushing the girl's long blonde hair.

"Welcome to California," she said, extending her hand. "Sorry we're late. Jennifer insisted on coming too and I had to pick her up from school—then she insisted on changing before coming to meet you. Say hello to Manisha, honey."

Jennifer came forward and handed me a small bunch of red oleanders. I thanked her and tried to shake her hand, but she disappeared behind her mother.

"Is this all of your luggage?" Mrs. Wallace asked. She began to wheel the cart through the exit.

Once in the car I relaxed, but felt even more tired. The forty-minute drive seemed interminable. Mrs. Wallace called my attention to various points of interest—buildings, museums, hospitals, parks. "Here is the largest park in the city. It includes a magnificent zoo. We'll have to bring you here as soon as you're rested. Right, Jenny?"

"Mommy," said Jennifer, moving up to the back of our seats, "where will Thomas sleep if she sleeps in the guest room?"

"Thomas is our cat," said Mrs. Wallace to me. "He likes to sleep on the guest room bed. Do you mind? I've heard that Indian people are not that keen on animals. Is that true? Sit back, Jenny, you'll hurt yourself."

I did not feel much like talking about Indian people and animals, but I did want to tell her that sharing a bed with Thomas, even if he were only a cat, was not something I would choose. It was, at least, true of people in India that their pets do not sleep in the same bed with them. But before I could say anything the car had entered the driveway of a huge ranch-style house with a three-car garage. The driveway was lined with bushes of red oleander. We stopped at the front door to unload the bags, and then dragged them to the guest room, next to the living room. I was relieved to see there was no cat on the bed.

"Would you like anything to eat or drink?" Mrs. Wallace asked. "Dinner won't be for over an hour."

"Yes, thank you, Mrs. Wallace," I said. "I'd like a glass of water, please. I'm not hungry. If it's all right with you, I'd like to skip dinner and go to bed. I'm so tired and sleepy—must be the jet-lag."

"Please call me Joyce. I feel I know you already. I feel good vibes from you. It's perfectly okay for you to sleep through tonight. Don't worry about a thing. You can meet Jim and John tomorrow at breakfast." She stepped out and returned in a minute with a glass of ice water. "Sleep well. Yell if you need anything. Lock the door if you don't want a visitor tonight." She winked before leaving.

"Good night and thank you for everything, Joyce," I said. Jennifer stood there for a few more seconds before following her mother.

I was pleased to have an attached bath, fully equipped with fresh towels and soap. After a hot shower I felt clean and ready for bed. I had not forgotten to lock the door.

* * *

I awoke in the grey light of early morning. The ceiling was not that of my Calcutta home. A quilt of geometric design, whose pattern I had never seen before, covered the warm bed. Vaguely, I recalled that I was in another country, not in familiar surroundings. I opened my eyes wider. The clock at the bedside read four. On the dresser across the room was a framed photograph of two children and a cat: I was in California, in the guest room of the Wallace family.

I rose, feeling fully awake, and suppressed an impulse to calculate the time in Calcutta. I knew it was long past morning there. I opened the venetian blinds to peer out. It was still dark. Street lamps glowed through the fog. My room looked out on the driveway. I had a desire to go outside and explore the area. The fog bestowed a look of mystery on what had seemed quite ordinary a few hours before. I had not known that California had fog as in the hills of Assam. Of course, I thought, one might expect it in a coastal town.

Suddenly I was hungry, very hungry. I had eaten nothing since breakfast in Hawaii the day before. I put on a bathrobe and slowly opened the door. There was no sound except the faint hum of a refrigerator. Following the hum to its source, I located the kitchen, beyond a formal dining room. I opened the huge refrigerator.

"Meow." Something furry touched my ankle, startling me. It must be Thomas, I thought, hungry after his nocturnal adventures. On two shelves of the refrigerator were cartons of yogurt —in rows—peach, orange, strawberry, even mango. On another shelf were half of a melon and a few cartons of cottage cheese. I did not feel like cold fruit or yogurt early on a foggy morning. Were the Wallaces a family of staunch vegetarians? Perhaps they thought I was. I recalled what I had heard about Californians— the Wallaces could easily be "health food freaks." I closed the refrigerator.

I heard a small crunching noise and found Thomas eating from a plate on the floor of a pantry. Good, I thought, perhaps I can find something here, some bread or cookies maybe. But the shelves held only cans and bags with pictures of cats on them. In this house a cat had better luck finding something to eat than a guest did, it seemed. I went back to my room.

I had bought a bar of chocolate when the plane from Calcutta had stopped in Singapore. It was still in my handbag, where I now went in search of it. Thomas had quietly followed me and was now securely in the bed, in the place where I had been only minutes earlier. He looked very content and satisfied, and closed his eyes. By the time I found my chocolate bar, the cat was fast asleep—a half-moon bundle of fur. I opened the blinds again, bit into the chocolate, and watched the California sun rise slowly through the fog, beyond the hazy street lamps.

I must have dozed off. A knock on the door woke me. "Are you up yet?" came my host's voice.

"Yes. Please come in." I was gazing at the oblique ray of sun on the carpet when a pair of pale bare feet with painted toe-nails moved into view. I looked up to see Joyce standing in front of me—without any clothes. I was now wide awake.

"Good morning," she said. "The sun is out. Isn't it lovely? It can be quite foggy around here all morning. You've brought the tropical sun, I think. I see Thomas found his way in. How about some breakfast?"

"Good morning," I answered, with my eyes averted. "I would love some breakfast, thank you."

Joyce left for the kitchen. So she was not going for a swim or anything like that. Was this the usual practice here? What about the rest of the family? Mr. Wallace? I got up from the sofa, washed my face, and changed from my robe to some real clothes.

When I got to the kitchen table, Jim Wallace was at its head, leafing through a newspaper and drinking his coffee. Jennifer was sitting next to a boy slightly older than her, who was John. They were eating cereal and talking. Joyce was at the counter, preparing toast. Everyone but Joyce was fully dressed and seemed unaware of her unclothed existence.

"Good morning, everyone." I said, trying to sound normal. Jim Wallace lowered the paper from his face and stood up.

"Good morning," he said. "Have you slept well? Sorry I have to rush—I've got an eight o'clock meeting. See you later. Enjoy your stay. I'm sure Joyce will show you around." After giving Jennifer a peck on the cheek, and ruffling the boy's hair gently, he hurried out. Not a word or gesture to his wife, I noticed.

"How do you like your tea, Manisha?" asked Joyce. "With milk, or black? Sugar? Would you rather have herbal tea?" I felt like saying I like my tea with clothes on. For some reason it seemed sacrilegious to stand naked in front of the stove.

"With milk, please. I can make it myself if you like." I was trying to be helpful—or perhaps to bring a sense of normalcy to the kitchen.

"Sure, help yourself," said Joyce. "We've got all flavors of yogurt. But you may want a hot breakfast, eggs and toast or such."

"That's a great idea. I'll make some eggs. Actually, I'm very hungry. I woke up early this morning and came looking for food. Did you hear me in the kitchen?"

"You must be famished," said Joyce. "I should have shown you where to find stuff for snacks. You see, I don't eat those things myself. I'm on a macrobiotic diet. Jim is the other extreme, a meat-and-potato man. And the kids will eat anything. So you get every kind of food in this house."

I wanted to ask what "macrobiotic" was, but decided to concentrate on making a hearty breakfast. The children got up, leaving half-finished bowls of cereal on the table. John pulled on his backpack and headed for the door, but Joyce ran after him with his lunch and gave him a hug. She then combed her daughter's long tresses and tied them in a rubber band. Jennifer kissed her mother and said goodbye to me.

"It's the next-door neighbor's turn to give the little kids a ride this morning," said Joyce when Jennifer had gone. "We carpool. I wanted this morning free to be with you." She gathered the dishes from the table.

"Thank you," I said, as I finished my breakfast. "That's very nice of you. I'd like to see the campus and find out about dorms and so forth."

"I'm going to take a quick dip in the pool first," she said, walking out to the patio. "Do you want to join me? The campus offices won't be open until ten. We can leave by nine or nine-thirty."

"No, thanks," I said, rising, and followed her to the door. "I think I'll wait till later for a swim. Maybe in the afternoon. You go ahead."

Joyce had stacked the dishes near the sink. I took the opportunity to wash them, though I realized there must be a dishwasher. I wanted to be useful. Something about this family was strange—and sad, at the same time. I began to feel sorry for Joyce. Her nudity seemed to bother me less already, as long as I was not expected to behave as she did. The children seemed at ease with it. I could not be sure about the husband. She is so friendly and helpful, I thought. It must be my own inhibitions. I was almost envious of her easy-going manner. She was quickly making me feel at home.

When we were ready to leave, Joyce took me around the house. She was now fully clothed. I was struck by the size of the bedrooms. Most impressive was Joyce's bathroom. Not only did it have magenta carpeting, wall-to-wall, but the fixtures were all similarly colored as well. There was a huge circular bathtub in the center of the room. I was astounded to see a magenta telephone on the wall next to the toilet.

"I have never seen a telephone in a bathroom before," I commented, unable to help myself.

"You find them more and more here as new homes are built," she said, taking my incredulity in stride. "It's actually very convenient. My friends call me all hours of the day or night. Let's go to the pool this way." She led me through a narrow corridor that ran from her bathroom directly out to the swimming pool.

Outside, she told me that she preferred not to wear anything around the house because her skin needed to breathe fresh air. Also, she wanted her children to be brought up seeing adults naked and natural. Jim, of course, did not agree with her on this. It was not only Jim, though. The neighbor behind them was very weird, she told me. He kept looking at her through the fence when she sunbathed or swam. He had come from Italy not too long ago, she said, adding that he must be some sort of pervert.

"So, feel free to take your clothes off around here. No one'll mind."

"Thanks. I feel quite comfortable with my clothes on. Besides, it's a bit chilly for me. I had no idea that September in California could be so cool."

"It is in the shade. Wait till you're in the sun."

We spent most of the day running errands and picking up information. We learned a lot about both on-campus and off-campus housing. I had a feeling that I should move as soon as possible, preferably to a small studio of my own. Adjusting to Joyce's unconventional ways might not be that easy, no matter how much I might admire her, I thought.

In the car Joyce began to talk about her marriage. I knew something like this would come, because she obviously lacked a sense of discretion—and made no distinction between private and public matters. She told me how Jim's values and hers were worlds apart. He didn't care a bit about natural living, nutrition, and friendship. He was set in his ideas and was interested only in his career and making money. Sure, he had provided Joyce and the kids with all the comforts imaginable. But she would have liked to share her life with him a bit more.

"What do you think, Manisha? Do you think he respects my ideas? What's your impression?"

"Joyce, I saw him barely a couple of minutes. It's hard to have an impression in such a short time." I didn't know how to handle the subject.

"You saw how he totally ignored me," she persisted. "Not even a goodbye."

"How do you think he feels about your inviting a total stranger into the house? Is he also part of the organization that welcomes foreign students?" It was a question that had been on my mind since morning.

"Oh, that's no problem," countered Joyce. "He gives me full freedom about the way I want to live. He is very supportive that way. Or, maybe indifferent is the word. I can invite anyone anytime, as long as Jim doesn't have to be involved. Sometimes I wonder if he isn't having an affair." She paused a moment. "Even with the kids, he is never really there. He just buys things." Joyce stopped, looking rather emotional and upset.

Despite my sympathy I began to feel very uncomfortable. I had no idea that being a guest for a week meant being a confidante. My natural curiosity about people's lives made it easier for me to be pulled into such conversations. But with Joyce, I had no way of telling how far this involvement might take me. Later, I came to realize that sharing such personal matters with a stranger was not unusual for a Californian to do. It was part of the ethos of "open communication," and not necessarily a sharing of confidence.

The thought of finding my own place as soon as possible became firmer in my mind. In the afternoon, after a lunch of wild rice, bean sprouts, tofu, and yogurt, I took a nap. My jet-lag had not entirely lifted yet. I felt better after the nap and unpacked a few things. I gave Joyce the silk piece I had bought for her. She was visibly pleased.

For the next few days I looked for an apartment. Joyce was very helpful. She drove me around a lot, along with her usual chauffeuring of the children to various places: Jennifer to school every other day, John to after-school basketball games, clarinet practice, and math tutorials. I was impressed by the amount of driving a typical housewife in America did. Joyce seemed to do it all with grace and without complaint. She seemed infinitely patient with the children. They were almost never disciplined. I saw Jim Wallace rarely, since I did not get up early enough to have breakfast with them, and in the evenings I would eat early, then go to bed to be alone and read a bit. Since I was hearing so much about his marriage, I felt uncomfortable facing him. Even when we ran into each other he did not initiate any conversation. In his eyes I must have been another of Joyce's passing whims.

That week I answered an ad placed by a chemistry student who wanted to share a cottage close to the ocean. I liked her open and relaxed approach to things. She said I could move in as soon as I was ready. I liked the place so much that I put a deposit down immediately, promising to move in that Sunday. My classes would start a week later. This would give me just enough time to settle in. I was happy with the location and the view. The cottage was large enough for me to have some privacy. I already began to compose letters home, describing my room overlooking the wild rose bushes and only a few steps from the Pacific Ocean. The best part was the rent—only seventy-five dollars a month.

Joyce planned a party for me that Saturday. "It's nice of you to go to all this trouble," I told her. "But isn't it too much bother—and in such a short time?"

"No problem," she said with animation. "I'd like to introduce you to some of my friends. They're hip—you'll love them. It will be no sweat, really—a pool-side, potluck party. We'll do some neat things, you'll see."

I was so grateful that I volunteered to make an Indian dish. The idea of a pool party with "hip" friends of Joyce scared me slightly. I did not dare ask about the dress-code. I was in such a good mood that I could accept whatever might happen. *When in California....*

On the night before the party, Joyce told me that Jim would be away for the weekend on a business trip to Palm Springs. "It's for the better. He doesn't enjoy my friends anyway. May I ask you a favor, Manisha?"

"Of course. What is it?"

"Would you wear a sari tomorrow? Not many people here have seen real Indian women in real Indian costume. It would be a treat."

"I was thinking of doing just that," I told her, which was the truth.

On Saturday, Joyce helped me shop for ingredients for the dish I planned to make. I insisted on paying for them. The dish was to be *raita,* a salad of yogurt and raw cucumbers. Joyce stood by in the kitchen that afternoon, helping put it together. Then she took John and Jennifer to a neighbor's house, where they would spend the night. When she returned, it was time to dress for the party, and Joyce asked if she could watch me drape the sari.

"Wow!" she said, amazed, as I showed her how it was done. "How do you ever keep it from slipping off? I could never keep it on." She herself wore a denim jumper.

"I suppose it's a matter of practice. After a while it becomes second nature." I assured her that there were no special tricks involved.

"We'll see," she said, and winked slightly, hurrying to answer the front door. The guests had begun to arrive.

By four most of Joyce's friends had come. They had gone immediately to the pool. Some sat on the edge, drinking iced tea, wine, or beer. Others took off their clothes and jumped in. I thought I detected a pair of eyes through the fence. Joyce kept warning me that there would be a great surprise for me later in the evening. One of the rooms in the house had been readied for that purpose. I was asked not to go there yet.

About twenty people, mostly couples, gathered around the buffet table with its assortment of food: many kinds of salads—salads with seeds and even flowers. I had a hard time recognizing the people I had seen at the pool now that they were dressed. Though I was not drinking, I felt dizzy in this loose and vague atmosphere. No one seemed interested in conversation. Few introductions were made. After a "Hi, how're you doin'?" they scattered in different directions.

We served ourselves on paper plates and ate with plastic forks and spoons, sitting wherever we found places to sit. One man stuffed spoonfuls of *raita* into his mouth. He was still in his swimming trunks, dripping all over the furniture. It seemed incongruous. "Gee, Joyce, it's good stuff." That was the extent of compliments on the *raita,* said by a few of the nameless women. Some of them stood around me, asking how I draped the sari. "Is it tailored like that?" they asked. No one seemed interested in the new dish they were served—or in much else, for that matter. I had to convince myself that this must be a very special crowd—at the university I would meet serious and interesting people.

After dinner, all the paper plates and plastic ware and other waste were quickly dumped into a large garbage bag. "Now is the time for the surprise," whispered Joyce into my ear, and disappeared in the direction of her bedroom.

"Friends, please come to the room with the sign Wonderland on it." came Joyce's voice over the intercom, a few minutes later.

In the week I had been there I had not heard anyone use the intercom. Nor had I explored the other rooms of the house. I had kept away from the area of Joyce's bedroom since the day she told me about her marital problems. Once she asked me to help with Jennifer's hair. On the way to Jennifer's room I had passed John's. It was cluttered with sports equipment, comic books, sneakers, and musical instruments. There were large posters of rock singers. Jennifer's room was a lot neater, with a double bed covered with stuffed animals in various sizes: teddy bears, monkeys, dogs, cats, even a snake. One wall had a built-in stereo system. Another wall had a walk-in closet full of clothes. I could not believe my eyes. So many clothes for a six-year-old!

Now we all walked down the hall, passing the children's rooms, entering still another part of the house. A door on our left bore a sign reading WONDERLAND. A faint smell of incense emerged from the room. Joyce stood inside the half-open door, wearing the silk piece I had given her. She wore it in a wrapped-towel fashion—held by her left shoulder—exposing her right breast and quite a bit of her left thigh. The material was only a yard wide and three yards long, not enough to wear as an Indian sari—or as a Roman toga. So, I wondered, is this the surprise?

"How about it, eh?" said Joyce, giving me a hug. This movement loosened the silk from her shoulder and it dropped in a sleek pile at her feet. Men clapped in enthusiasm. The women smiled knowingly.

"Give me a belt or a string," I said, picking up the silk and trying to tie it around her bare body. "I can help you."

"Thanks, Manisha. I don't know how you keep that thing on yourself so long." A young man took off his own belt and handed it to me. I managed to hoist the silk on her shoulder again. A breast remained uncovered. The dim blue light of Wonderland made it less noticeable.

Why was I so squeamish? I had seen plenty of bare-breasted women in tribal India. What was the big fuss, anyway? After all, I had been seeing Joyce's naked body every morning for a week. The words of a famous Bengali author flashed through my mind.

A savage is beautiful in the wild just as a baby is in its mother's arms.

Now fairly secure in her silk sarong, Joyce settled on a beanbag chair in the middle of the carpeted room, which had no other furniture but large pillows. "Hello, everyone," she said. "Welcome to Wonderland. I've a great surprise for all of you wonderful people. Tonight we'll show my new friend from India how we Californians are free to enjoy ourselves. I suggest we pair off with the person next to us and touch each other everywhere, nicely and gently, with love and affection. I also suggest that it would be easier if we take off our clothes. Feel free. It's a wonderful feeling to be able to touch another human being with freedom and love. Right?"

"*Right,*" voices resonated in unison through the room. I saw trouble.

"Come on, Manisha," said Joyce. "You can begin with me, if you're shy." The young man who sacrificed his belt earlier was still at my side. He took my wrist.

"Oh no, she's mine," he said. "I've never touched a saried woman before. Sorry, Joyce." He laughed at his own pun. Now I saw big trouble.

"Let me just go to my room for a second," I said. "I'll change into something simpler so that I'm more exposed. I'll be back in a minute." Before they could object I went out and closed the door. In my room I did change—into a pair of blue jeans and a sweater. I went back and quietly peeped in the door of Wonderland. I saw that everyone was touching someone else. Joyce had lost her silk piece again and the young man without a belt had lost his pants. They were doing more than touching. The room looked like a tub of seething white and tanned flesh. I closed the door before my undigested salad had a chance to come up.

I left the house and walked out into the cool evening. After about an hour I turned back. It was getting cold. All the cars were still in the driveway. I tiptoed into the house, went to the kitchen, and dished out some leftover *raita*. I sat on a stool in the pantry to eat. Thomas came and rubbed his jaw against my ankle. Tonight I might even let him sleep in my bed above the quilt, I thought. It would be easier to do this than to participate in the Wonderland party. Thank God it is far enough from my room. I can sleep without any disturbance. Thank God I leave tomorrow. I reminded myself to apologize to Joyce in the morning.

* * *

I saw Joyce again in November. We had lunch and she told me that she was having an affair with a Mexican-American construction worker. Jim had asked her for a divorce. The news did not surprise me.

I have mixed feelings for Joyce. I admire her natural friendliness and lack of inhibition—as long as I don't have to live that way. But then, Joyce never pushed me to conform to her ways. I cannot help feeling sympathetic toward someone whose totally unselfconscious behavior made her unique even among the free-spirited Californians. I find it hard to judge her.

— *1969* —

Liberated Linda

"What's your sign?"

I was being pressed up against the kitchen sink by a houseful of people. A young man stood at my side, his long blond hair in a beaded headband, holding an open container of yogurt and gazing expectantly at me.

The year was 1969, the place, La Jolla. I had moved back to America after four years in India. The country had changed in the meantime. One heard a lot now about rallies and "liberation." I wasn't sure if it were happening only in California.

Linda, my new roommate, had invited me to this Friday night bash hosted by a group of our fellow students. "You need to meet the people here," she had said. "It's not like your old campus in the boondocks of the Midwest. We are really on the cutting edge of things. Come along."

So I came along, and thus far had tried to "go with the flow," though without much success, ending up against the sink and the young man with the beaded headband.

"I beg your pardon?" I said, raising my voice in the din, not sure I had heard him right. "My sign?"

He came even closer, and held in offer before my eyes a spoon dripping with yogurt. I shrank back. "I mean your *sign,*" he said, putting the spoon into his own mouth.

Now I was alarmed. Could he be alluding to something sexual? My experience with the Californians so far had made one thing clear. They were open, wide open—not only in their speech, but in other ways as well—to anything.

Another wave of people moved into the kitchen, pushing me away from the young blond man. I spotted Linda a few heads to my right and followed her out of the kitchen. Once in the hallway, I told her of the question about my sign.

"Oh, that must be Terry," she laughed. "He's into astrology and wants to know your *zodiac* sign. Everyone knows you Indians have horoscopes from day one."

She moved down the hall and entered another room. I looked back toward the kitchen, but the door was totally blocked by people. I couldn't see the blond hair with the headband at all. I supposed I did not have to kill myself to find him only to say that I did not have a horoscope and had no idea what my sign was.

I turned again in the direction Linda had gone, to tell her I was ready to leave. The crowd, the cigarette smoke, and the noise were getting on my nerves. I had seen no food or drink except the young man's yogurt and a huge bowl of crushed potato chips on a corner table.

Inside the room where Linda had gone, the crowd was smaller. Ten or twelve people sat on the floor in a ring. The blinds were drawn and I could smell incense and hear soft music. Curious, I stood in the doorway. A bearded man, slightly older than the rest, kneeled over a wooden sculpture, a life-size bust of an African. He turned the head this way and that as if he were trying to break its neck. After a moment, the head came off its shoulders. Holding it in one hand, he put his other hand up inside the neck and took out a small plastic bag. I thought he was entertaining his guests with some kind of magic show.

I almost forgot that I was looking for Linda. In the dim light it was hard to find her. The bearded man came toward me, pulled me in, and closed the door. I had no choice but to sit in the ring with the others. The master of ceremonies now sat on the floor next to the beheaded African sculpture and opened the plastic bag. He began to roll thin cigarettes from the leafy contents. I spotted Linda on the other side of the room. I crawled quietly around the outside of the circle and whispered to her that I really wanted to go home. Perhaps she could find a ride with someone else. Before she could say anything, the woman on her left passed me a half-smoked cigarette. I took it and passed it on to Linda.

"Come on, have a puff," she said. Her eyes were imploring. "It's great stuff. Roger smuggled it in from Turkey last month. It will liberate you, Manish."

I did not respond, but crawled back toward the door. I committed the sacrilege of not participating at my own initiation to the cult of smoking and liberation. I could have tasted the "great stuff" if I had not had a bad headache already. Maybe another time, I said to myself. *When in California....* Right now I needed to go home and catch up on some reading for Monday's class.

Next morning I woke up early, something I never did in Rochester or Chicago. It must have been the ocean air and California sun, though the sun did not show up until afternoon, at least on this stretch of coast. I had my breakfast alone and went for a walk along the cove. The morning mist was lingering, making the water and land hard to tell apart.

I have always liked fog. In Assam, where I lived as a child, there are morning and evening fogs during the winter months. It is as if the hills were wrapped in a muslin cloth. I remember weaving many fantasies about what might be hidden by the fog—a castle, perhaps, with a sleeping princess in it. Now the California fog began to lift, and the gulls started a terrible racket. I turned back.

* * *

I thanked my good fortune to have met Linda, who offered me this luxury of being so close to the ocean. When I answered her ad on a campus bulletin board for a roommate, I had no idea that the place would be so charming. I fell in love with it—a white cottage with a red-tiled roof—the moment I saw it. A tiny front lawn was almost covered with a hedge of wild roses. Although I was first reminded then of the castle of the Sleeping Beauty, Linda herself seemed quite awake, in a spacy California way. Does she have a prince, I wondered, to brave the tangled thorns?

The inside of the cottage was not as enchanting as the outside, however. We shared the only bathroom, which was next to Linda's bedroom. My room was on the other side of the cottage, across the living area, between the front door and the tiny kitchen. But beyond the kitchen was a lovely little porch, and a backyard where Linda kept a hibachi.

I was struck by Linda's friendliness when we first met. A short while before, I had had a taste of California hospitality and was now cautious. But Linda disarmed me.

"I've always been interested in India," she told me. "I've admired Indira Gandhi ever since I first heard about her. Without a doubt, she is the most liberated woman in the world. Now I can learn more about that fabulous country from you." A twinge of nostalgia hit me when she talked like that.

"Oh, by the way," she continued, "I also love Indian food. Would you teach me a few simple recipes? Oh, wait—I've a great idea. We'll throw a party and serve Indian food. Won't that be fun?" Her face glowed.

"Sure," I began, "why not?" She put her arms around me in a sudden display of warmth that embarrassed me a bit. I felt I would be a cold fish not to respond to her invitation of instant friendship. I tried to cover my awkwardness. "I do like to cook. Maybe we can have our first Indian meal as soon as I move in."

"It's a deal." She put her hand out to shake mine. I had never seen a woman do that before. I was impressed.

So, the day after I moved in, I went shopping for whatever ingredients I could find in the nearby supermarket. I prepared a simple Indian meal, hoping to surprise Linda. She did not come home that evening. Perhaps she has one of her labs, I thought. Linda was majoring in Chemistry and had already warned me that her class and lab schedules were at all sorts of strange hours. But when she did not show up by dinner time, I felt a bit disappointed. Should she not have called to say that she would be late? I had never lived with a roommate before. Wasn't it like a family living together? I ate alone, and put the leftovers away in various plastic containers, thinking they would be much tastier the next day. Exhausted, I went to bed around midnight.

A sound woke me up. The little clock next to my bed showed two a.m. I got up when I heard voices in the kitchen. It was Linda, feeding spoonfuls of my curry to a man whom I had never seen before. They were having great fun laughing, talking, and eating. They had not heard me come. I stood in the door, watching the disappearance of the shrimp and the potatoes, one by one, into the mouth of a stranger. Something about it disturbed me enough that I hurried back to my room, but I could not fall asleep for a long time.

Next day, I discovered that Linda had not bothered to leave a note or anything to tell me that they'd eaten the food. There was not a grain left. I argued with myself that she took our "deal" seriously and had presumed that I left the food for her. But didn't she like it? I thought Americans say "thank you" all the time.

I did not see Linda for a week. Her schedule did appear quite hectic, as she had already warned me it would be. In a way, I welcomed the time alone in the house, finding my way around, getting settled. Because of the late-night curry incident, I decided not to cook anymore large quantities of food.

One Sunday morning I ran into Linda in the kitchen, standing by the window in her robe. She had on a pair of earphones and kept bobbing her head slightly while she drank her coffee and read the newspaper. I had to admire her dexterity. I made my tea and went out to the back porch. It was a lovely warm morning, now that the early fog was gone.

"Hey, Manish," Linda called from the kitchen, "Want to go to hear Gloria Steinem? She'll be on the campus this afternoon."

"Who is Gloria Steinem?"

"You don't know? Wow! You don't know the most important feminist leader in the world today? Where have you been, my friend?" She seemed really astounded by my ignorance.

"India," I said, trying to joke to cover my embarrassment. "Well, I'm not that political. Tell me about her."

"Oh, it's hard to describe her. She is my guru, my mentor, and my inspiration. She helped me and many women of my generation to see who we really are, to discover our power. No man can treat me as a sex-object—or any object—anymore. And you haven't even heard of her?" Linda kept shaking her head in disbelief. "You've got to see her for yourself, Manisha. She is *dynamite*. She is the best thing that happened to this country since John Kennedy, believe me." Linda stopped, her eyes glowing with pride. This was a side of Linda I hadn't seen. She was more serious than I had imagined her to be. At the same time, I envied her for such awareness at her age.

"I'd like to go," I said. "Where is it, and when?"

"I tell you what," she said, turning the paper around to check the exact place and time. "I told Tim that I would have lunch with him. I'll come by here around two-thirty and pick you up. There is no point both of us driving. Parking won't be easy."

That afternoon I stood in a crowd of a thousand students in the university quadrangle to listen to Linda's guru. I could barely see her from behind all the people. Her straight, shoulder-length, blonde hair fell freely around a bright face. Large-rimmed tinted glasses gave the face a dignity. Gloria Steinem talked about the liberation of women: how women must come together in a sisterhood and learn to value themselves, how women must have the courage to ignore much of what their fathers and mothers told them or what their boyfriends expected of them.

She said many fiery and impressive things. The words vibrated in the air, the same air we were barely breathing. The magnetism was palpable. After a while, however, I lost my concentration on the meaning of the words. All around me, faces, many kinds of faces—white, black, brown, Chinese, Japanese, Hispanic—all glowed with enthusiasm. The red light of the setting sun made them look very dramatic. I found it hard not to be infected by this special energy. I felt as if we were on the verge of a significant revolution.

Afterwards, Linda introduced me to some of her political friends. We all went to a cafe where we talked about the speech.

"Isn't she fantastic?"

"God, I wish I could get to know her."

"How about starting a women's group?" said a woman with short red hair. "Linda, how do you feel about it? You are the only one with a separate living room where we could meet."

"I have an idea," said another voice, whose face I could not see in the cigarette smoke. "We can all begin by telling our life stories and check out what exploitation went on in our lives. Then we'll know for sure what to do."

"Great idea," chimed in the red-haired speaker. She looked at me. "Would you like to join us? Won't it be interesting to hear how Indian women are exploited? I once saw a documentary on India where women covered their faces with their saries and walked behind the men. Gee, how do they tolerate such inequality in this day and age?"

A twinge of frustration began to rise inside me. I wanted to put some of these ideas in the right context. I wanted to explain that the situation in India was immensely complex. But I was not sure how to go about it. I opened my mouth to speak but the woman had already changed the topic.

"We all need to take a pledge that we don't need men for anything. It would be really fun to do without them and build our sisterhood, as Gloria Steinem suggested."

"Amen," several voices cried out together.

I began to feel tired and dizzy from the noise and smoke, which smelled not only of cigarettes but also of marijuana. I nudged Linda. "I don't feel too well. Could we go back, please?"

"What's the matter? Are you sick? Gee, you don't look too good. It's getting a bit crowded here for me, too." She turned to the others. "Okay, guys, we're off. Let's talk about the group over the phone some more. I'm game. Our living room will be available."

Back at the cottage I wanted to be alone—alone and away from all the talk, talk about liberation, equality, and all the rest. Something was not right. That night I went to bed early and did not sleep very well. I had fleeting dreams in which rows of American women were walking behind rows of veiled Indian women: a wish-fulfilling dream, no doubt.

Several weeks passed. One morning I was awakened very early by a sudden chill. It was that juncture of night and dawn when everything is quiet and cold. I tried to pull my blanket to the chin and sleep again. A rustling sound made me open my eyes. I saw a shadow outside my window: it was gently knocking on the pane. Quickly, I got up and went to the window. It was one of Linda's male friends.

He gestured to me to open the front door. I remembered then that Linda was with another man the previous evening and I hadn't seen him leave. I went to the door and said that Linda was not in. He wore a white coat, with a badge identifying him as a doctor.

"Oh, well," he said, slightly disappointed. "I thought of dropping in after my night-shift. Please tell her Tom came by. I'll call later today. Thanks." He walked away in tired steps.

That afternoon, I caught a glimpse of Linda taking her bike out for a ride. I told her about the early morning visitor.

"Thanks Manish," she said. "Thanks for not letting him in. I couldn't handle two of them at that hour. Not that it's any of his business. He does that—just drops in without calling. Thanks a million. I owe you one. You're a good friend." Linda stretched out her arms to hug me.

"It's none of my business either," I said. "But I'm confused... I thought you and your friends are trying to do without men." I had blurted out what was on my mind.

"Well, sure," replied Linda. "We're trying to be independent of men's expectations. That doesn't mean I don't love them. I seem to need a lot of intimacy. Sometimes I'm confused, too. It's not clear in my mind how to balance the two. Oops, I'm late. Let's continue this later. I'd like to hear your ideas on the subject. So long, and thanks again." She pushed her bike through the front door.

Our conversation lingered with me all day. For the first time in several weeks I saw Linda's dilemma more clearly. What was this liberation exactly, for which Linda and other women were aspiring? Why was this not such a burning issue for me? I was busy managing my meager fellowship and trying to finish my graduate studies as soon as I could. How come I was not involved in such important problems? I needed to have a serious discussion with Linda and her friends about this.

A few days passed. One foggy morning I took my ocean walk and returned, composing in my mind the outline of a term paper. I found Linda in the kitchen making coffee.

"Good morning, Linda. How have you been?"

"Oh, hi. I'm fine. I'm glad you're up," she declared. "How'd you like to have a party? Remember our talk about cooking Indian food? I'm thinking of inviting my girl friends. You met most of them after Gloria Steinem's speech." Linda moved out of the kitchen to the back porch. I followed, thinking I did not want to cook for hours for women I did not know well or like enough.

"That sounds like a great idea," I said. "But why don't we do a potluck? I'd be happy to make one dish, you can make one, and the others could bring the rest. This way no one will feel overworked or exploited." I stressed the last word.

"I was thinking more like a party to decide on our women's group," she replied. "Won't it be fun to brainstorm over delicious shrimp curry and rice? Boy, was that curry good! Tim still talks about it."

"Does he?" I said. "Well, maybe we should invite him and a few other men to hear our brainstorming, then help us clean up afterwards. It's time men helped in the kitchen, don't you think?"

"Oh, I meant to tell you, Manish. Please don't mention a word about Tim or any of my boyfriends to the girls. They don't know

THE WEST COAST CROWD

about my private life and they don't need to know. You understand, don't you?" I was stunned into silence. It appeared safer to change the topic altogether.

"If you're thinking of an all-girl party, it's okay with me," I said. "But I don't have time to make all the food. I'd be glad to make a shrimp curry, if you help me. Someone else can make rice and another can make salad. We don't need many dishes to brainstorm over." I was firm. I was not going to become one of their veiled Indian women, to be exploited.

"Okay. That sounds fine," said Linda. "Keep next Saturday free."

"One more thing," I said. "You and I split the cost of the dish we make—we'll go shopping together at nine on Friday morning." I was impressed by my own directness.

"Sure, no problem." Linda seemed in a hurry to depart. She must be running a lab experiment again, I thought, as she headed out the door.

I considered our conversation for a moment. I hoped I had not come on too strong. With Linda and many of my acquaintances here, I was never sure if they were just being careless in their speech. In India, when I encountered strangers, the cues were never mixed. Words were often unnecessary. Here, even with a lot of verbal communication, I was left wondering. It seemed the longer I spent in a new culture, the less I understood it.

The next Friday, I woke early to catch Linda and take her shopping. She did not appear at the appointed hour—so typical of her, not to take her promises seriously. Annoyed, I knocked on her bedroom door. No answer. The door was unlocked. I opened it a bit to see if she had left for the day. The bike would be the signal. A man was sound asleep in the bed, but the bike was there as usual. So where was she? There was nothing I could do at that point. So I left instead for the library. On the way home that afternoon, I picked up several pounds of shrimp and other ingredients. Linda had not bothered to tell me how many women were expected. After shelling and marinating the shrimp, I went to my room and did some work before turning in.

The next day I woke up late, the usual Saturday routine with me, so as to catch up on the sleep lost during the week. After breakfast I decided to pick up around the house and to clean the bathroom. There would be at least a dozen women for the party that evening, I figured. The bathroom was steamed up when I went into it with a pail and a mop. Had Linda come in to take a quick shower when I was in the kitchen? When my eyes got accustomed to the steam, I saw the pale naked body of a man floating in the bathtub. A muffled scream escaped from my throat. The dead man opened his eyes.

"Oh, hi," he said. "Do you want to use the john? Go right ahead." I ran back to the living room, wondering if this were the same man I saw in bed the day before. He did not look like Tim, who ate my shrimp, or the doctor, Tom, whom I dissuaded from coming in that early morning. Anyway, his identity was not my concern right now. I went to the bathroom door, but did not enter.

"Excuse me," I called. "Do you know where Linda is? Did she say when she'd be back?"

"Yeah," he replied. "Linda left for L.A. this morning. She had to meet an old boyfriend who just came back from Vietnam. She didn't say when she'd be back."

"What? L.A.? Are you sure?"

"Yup." From the splashing, I could tell that he was climbing out of the tub. I removed myself quickly, not knowing what to think or do.

When I calmed down a bit I had to consider that Linda could not be that irresponsible. I began to look everywhere for a note from her, without avail. Either the party was canceled or she would show up in a few hours. But what about her responsibility toward me? The party was supposed to be our joint venture. I began to get angry. Despite all my brave efforts I had become the victim of exploitation after all.

Meanwhile, the man emerged from the bathroom in blue jeans and a T-shirt with a Native American head on the chest.

"Could I have some coffee, please?" he asked with a smile. "Do you have any bagels or danish?" It made me even more furious.

"Help yourself," I said. "The kitchen is on your left, through that door. I don't know about bagels or danish. I don't eat them. There may be some frozen ones." I began to walk out to avoid him, but stopped.

"Do you remember her saying anything," I asked, "like she may not come back tonight, or about a party?" My desperation was obvious.

Seeing him a bit puzzled, I realized that we hadn't bothered to introduce ourselves. "I'm Manisha," I said, managing a smile.

"And I'm Barry," he replied. "Well, I was half asleep when she left. So I can't really remember if she said anything. You mean you have a party to go to tonight? If she doesn't show up I'd be happy to come with you."

"No, no," I said. *"We're* going to give a party. Now I'm not so sure anymore."

I followed Barry to the kitchen without thinking why. Perhaps I wanted to be reassured by the only human connection with Linda at hand. He made some coffee and offered me a mug as well. He seemed quite relaxed after a few sips.

"Why don't you have the party anyway?" he said. "If she appears, it'll be a nice surprise. I could help. It would be fun. Will you make some Indian goodies?"

"I don't think I'm in the mood for a party anymore. You see, it was not my idea to begin with. Thanks for the offer, anyway."

"Well, whatever," said Barry, as he put the coffee mug in the sink. He took the rubber band from the rolled newspaper at the door and put it around his long hair. "Bye now. Let me know if you change your mind. Here is my number." He wrote a telephone number on the newspaper and left.

I sat at the kitchen table for at least an hour, trying to understand the whole situation. It was not clear if all this was normal California behavior or simply typical of Linda. Given her lifestyle, anything seemed possible. Now, who was Barry? A lover, or just a friend? He seemed perfectly relaxed about her going to see an old boyfriend in another town, leaving him half asleep in her bed. I needed relief from these people. What was next? Just wait until afternoon and see what happens? What about all the shrimp?

"Freeze them," an inner voice said. Good idea. This way, if Linda showed up at the last moment, she couldn't have a party of Indian shrimp curry. The first possibility of revenge tasted sweet. An hour later I left again for the library, something I rarely did on a Saturday. I did not want to be around if any of the guests arrived.

I spent the whole afternoon and early evening at the library, and got a lot of reading done. I had a hamburger at the campus cafeteria before leaving for home. I rehearsed my arguments with Linda one more time as I approached the house.

I could not find my usual parking place. A number of cars were parked on the road and in the back alley. Was the party going on without us?

When I approached the house I saw a man standing next to the wild rose hedge, closing his fly. He was startled to see me and stammered, "The bathroom is occupied, so I..." He then followed me into the house—and into my room.

"I'm hiding here for the evening," he said. "Linda doesn't want me to go in there. This must be your room. Sorry about the trespassing. I have been enjoying reading the volume of Sanskrit poetry. I wish I could go to her room without being seen."

This time I could not summon the courtesy to introduce myself to this new stranger. I burst into the living room and saw about ten women, sitting everywhere, and Linda, who was cutting a large pizza.

"Here you are, Manish," she said. "We were getting worried about you. When I saw no shrimp curry, I figured you forgot. So we ordered a pizza. Come join us. It'll be only seventy cents per person. It's cheap and no work. That's the way. We women think we have to break our backs cooking meals for everyone else." She handed me a triangular piece with strings of cheese hanging between it and the mother pizza.

"Linda, may I talk to you alone for a second, please?" I dragged her to the kitchen. "Who is this man in my room? You leave for L.A. without a word, then appear without a warning and put a strange man in my room. Don't you have the minimum of sense to..." I was too angry to continue.

"Oh, him?" she responded. "He's a friend of my old boyfriend. He'll be in your room only until the party is over. I didn't think you'd mind if they were told he's your date or guest or something. You Indians are unpredictable anyway. So the girls won't wonder too much. Just for a few hours, please. And, I didn't go to L.A. I just told Barry that. He is so clinging, I had to get away somehow. I promised John that I would spend the day with him. We had the most fantastic picnic in Torrey Pines

Reserve[30]. You have to go there sometime. Well, let's not waste more time. Everyone is waiting."

I held Linda by the arm, but not as hard as I intended to. "Wait just a minute. Why are you hiding your men from these friends? What's the big problem?"

"Come on," she pleaded. "I don't want them to know that I'm dependent on men's attention and sex. Don't play dumb, Manish."

She freed herself from my clutch and went back to the living room. "Where were we?" she said to her friends.

I swallowed hard, went in to the party, and sat in a corner, keeping my eyes fixed on my room, trying to imagine what the man might be doing. He couldn't spend several hours reading translations of Sanskrit poetry. I couldn't concentrate on what the women were saying. An idea of my own shaped itself slowly but steadily. I knew now that I had to think seriously of moving out. It would be a pity. I loved the proximity to the ocean, the wild rose hedge, and my little room overlooking it.

Thinking of the rose hedge it occurred to me that no Linda could be awakened by a prince who used a hedge to relieve himself. In the California fairy tale of the late sixties, it would have to be a new breed of men to do the job, if at all.

By midnight, the women had left, thanking Linda for a wonderfully stimulating discussion toward forming a new cell of the women's liberation movement.

— *1969* —

---

[30] The rare Torrey pine grows only here and on the island of Santa Rosa. The tree is named after John Torrey, the 19th century U.S. botanist.

The Uninvited Informant

"This is Larry Sterling—I've heard from my ex that you've interviewed her," came the voice on the phone. "Don't you think you should talk to me also? After all, you're hearing only the one side." Actually, I was delighted by the opportunity, though the manner of contact was unconventional.

"I'm glad you feel this way," I said. "Yes, I'm very interested in hearing what you have to say on the subject. Would you be able to meet me at the Anthropology Department office next week sometime?"

"Why don't we meet at Black's Beach; say, at noon tomorrow, instead? You see, I'm running some very important lab tests. It might be hard for me to get away next week." Larry's ex-wife had told me that he was a microbiologist at the Institute of Oceanography.

"Why the beach?" I replied. "I don't really want to interfere with your lunch hour. Should we wait until you've more time?"

"I might not have more time. These tests may keep me busy around the clock for several weeks to come. At the beach, between swims, is the only place I can talk to you. I'll be relaxed enough to talk about things that are painful to me, things I don't usually enjoy talking about. So, bring your tape-recorder—and your swimsuit."

"Okay, I'll be there," I said, and considered that he was in a sense doing me a favor. "Where exactly shall I look for you?"

"Look for a big orange towel with Marilyn Monroe on it. I won't be far from it. It should be easy to spot me. I'm six-two and handsome." He hung up.

I began to have all sorts of misgivings. I really did not want to be pushed like this into an appointment. Also, the inappropriateness of the meeting-place could not be ignored. Now it was too late—and I had forgotten to ask for his telephone number. I argued with myself that I was in Southern California, not a West

Bengal village. When I asked a colleague for directions to Black's Beach, he looked very surprised, but gave them without comment.

This interview would continue a plan for research on divorce in Southern California, a part of my doctoral work. I wanted to study a segment of the technologically-advanced society of America. "I want to be the first anthropologist," I had told my professors, "to study the tribe no one else has, the white Anglo-Saxon American." They agreed that this would be an unusual venture.

My first plan, for research on the California rich, was quickly abandoned. I decided then to shift to divorce, a phenomenon that was now becoming a norm. What had made my first choice go awry was the watch dogs. These dogs, huge and ferocious, guarded the houses and property of the rich. They sprang at me with such vigor that my enthusiasm rapidly disappeared. This caused me to forsake my ambition to write the definitive work on the subject. I doubt if these dogs could have been appeased by Hercules himself, who had used all his tricks on the underworld Cerberus[31].

Meanwhile, many of my acquaintances were going through divorce. From the rich to divorce was not the most logical of shifts. Volumes had already been written on divorce. My research, however, would be different: a study of the points of view of the formerly married partners: How do the husband and wife experience, evaluate, and deal with the separation and divorce, over time? Is there any qualitative difference between their experience and their perception of it? If so, why? I had a hypothesis that each partner would evaluate the reasons and conditions of the divorce differently, partly because of their different expectations of marriage.

So, the rich were out and divorce was in, and so was I. I could not have picked a better topic. Every divorced person I knew—even barely—wanted to be my informant. I almost understood why the rich had their watch dogs. Within three days, I had made twenty appointments. How different this was from all the traditional problems of establishing rapport in the field! I wondered

---

[31] In Greek mythology, Cerberus was the great three-headed dog who guarded the entrance to the underworld.

what Malinowski might have said, had he written a study of contemporary California.

But the day after the call from Larry, while I was preparing for my appointment with him, my misgivings about the interview persisted. To begin with, I was not a beach person. My swimming endeavors were confined to Y.M.C.A. pools, and sunbathing was out of the question for a person from the tropics. Reluctantly, a little after twelve that afternoon, I found myself on Black's Beach.

I had to park the car up on the road and climb down to the beach through a canyon lined with gravel and thorns. I startled a napping lizard when I almost stepped on it. Could there, I wondered, be other reptiles in this canyon? Twice I lost my balance and nearly dropped the tape-recorder. There has to be a better path to the beach, I thought. My earlier misgivings now seemed like a premonition.

Finally I reached the sand. I realized with a shock that I was on a beach reserved for nude bathing. All my ambivalence toward the naked human body surfaced, and I lowered my eyes to the sand at my feet. I walked along like this, furtively looking for a towel with Marilyn Monroe on it. As I passed scores of running, walking, reclining bodies, I began to compose in my mind a paper which argued the necessity for the invention of clothes. My displeasure was mixed with curiosity, I have to admit, about the person I was to meet. What exactly, I wondered, does he have in mind?

I spotted a wrinkled Marilyn beneath a man lying naked on his stomach. I cleared my throat and he lifted his head slightly to squint at me.

"You're late," he said, perfunctorily. "Would you be sweet enough to rub some lotion on my back? I can't reach that far." He pointed to a plastic bottle.

"I'm here to interview you—at your suggestion," I said. "We haven't even said hello yet, and you're asking me to rub lotion on your back?"

"Well, then, hello there," said Larry, and rolled over. I looked away, having discovered one piece of truth: nudity was less embarrassing in a stranger than in someone I had just met. "If you want to ask me questions about my divorce," he continued, "we've got to establish a rapport, right? So, let's get acquainted."

He stretched out his hand with the bottle of lotion in it and gestured with his eyes to the empty portion of towel. I ignored him and sat on the sand. I could not bring myself to sit on Marilyn Monroe's thighs.

"Shall we get started?" I asked. Larry sat up, covering the lower part of his body with the towel. He seemed surprised at my matter-of-fact tone.

"Relax, lady," he said. "What's the big deal? Are you always this uptight?" Then he looked at his watch. "Oops, I've got to be going. Must look in on a lab test by one-fifteen. These are delicate organisms, you know. Look, since this is not the right place for you, why don't we meet for dinner tonight?" He got up and gathered his things. "I know a quiet place off the highway about five miles from here. I would have clothes on and you can ask me all the questions you want. It would be totally professional, I promise." He raised his right hand in pledge and began to walk away. Marilyn's body hung in folds around his. Annoyed, I had no choice but to follow.

"It was you who called *me* to talk," I called after him. "I was here to listen to you. Instead..." I waved my arm toward the crowded beach. "If you're still interested in telling me your side of the story, we meet in your office or mine." I began to wonder whether I was making a fool of myself. Did I need an informant so badly that I was pursuing a man who had so little sense of decorum? When we parted in the parking area, he got into his Corvette and saluted.

"See you soon," he said, and drove away.

Two days later, Larry telephoned again, asking if two p.m. the next day, at his office, would suit me. Relieved a little by the place of meeting, I agreed.

I arrived at his office as scheduled to find him on the phone, legs stretched out on the desk, his feet pointing toward the door. He raised his free hand in greeting without moving anything else. This time I noticed his greying temples and a tanned but handsome face. I couldn't be sure which side of forty he was. The telephone conversation went on for another five minutes. I tried not to overhear and not to get annoyed. The window of the office overlooked a patch of quiet blue ocean several hundred feet below. It looked like a painting.

"You have a lovely view," I offered, to begin our interview when Larry finally put down the receiver.

"Oh, yeah," he said, swiveling thirty degrees to face me across the desk. "I hardly notice it. But it's great to be so close to the beach. I can be there in less than five minutes. I take advantage of that in my lunch hour, unless I'm tied up with my work. Oh, I forgot. No mention of the beach." He crossed his heart.

"Shall we get started?" I responded, as I unpacked the tape-recorder.

"Hey, that's a beauty," he said. "Where did you get it? Japanese? Must be. May I?" I handed the machine over to him, getting slightly impatient at what seemed to be a determined effort to delay the interview. After a few minutes, he put the tape-recorder down, then raised himself from the chair. "Would you like some coffee?"

"No, thanks," I said, not able to show much annoyance with such a gesture. "So... what was it you wanted to tell me about your divorce?"

"Oh, that," he said. "But what's the rush? We're just getting to know..." But seeing my expression he changed his tone. "Let's see, where to start? Well, when I heard that Pam had three hours of tape telling you about me..." He sat down with his coffee.

"Why don't you just begin," I interrupted, "by telling me why you had to have a divorce? What went wrong—from your point of view, that is?" I pressed the button on the recorder.

"What went wrong? I'll tell you." For the first time, Larry's face took on a serious expression. It got increasingly red as he talked. "Two years ago, Pam decided to go back to school. Our youngest was in high school and she wasn't so busy with the kids anymore. I thought, Why not? Pam was a grade A student in college. If going back to school makes her happy, so be it. She could even work toward a Master's Degree and someday, when the kids are all grown, she could go back to work, part-time. I didn't ask her what courses she planned to take. For a while everything was going fine. I changed my schedule around a bit to accommodate hers, in case she had some school activity in the evenings."

Larry got out of his chair and walked toward the window, looked out at the ocean for a few minutes, then turned around. He began again, but firmer, louder.

"Occasionally Pam would tell me how excited she felt being back to school after all these years. Then, suddenly, about a year and a half later, there was a change in her. Her *language* seemed different. She used a lot of terms I'd never heard before. She told me that she was taking clinical psychology courses. In no time, she began to criticize me, using those terms. Soon I couldn't do anything right. It was no joke, believe me." Larry stopped and looked at me, as if trying to read my reactions.

"Mind you," he continued, "I was all for her education. I'd always been proud of Pam's academic achievements. She was a far better student than I could ever be. But this? The more courses she took, the further she got away from me—from *us,* the family. I still can't figure out how all this happened." His voice lost its strength when he uttered the last sentence. He refilled his coffee cup. He seemed anxious to go on.

"One day, after a major argument, I told her that she should forget her courses and stay home. She would be an easier person to live with. She burst out that I was not only a chauvinist pig, I was also the *most insensitive* of men, and I'd pay for this kind of cruelty. And before long she went to an attorney and filed for divorce. The whole thing was a nightmare. She even wanted me to go into therapy to improve myself. At any rate, to make a long story short, I fought like hell over custody of our youngest, and lost...."

Larry sat down again, and looked directly at me. "The system, the attorneys, and even the judge seemed to be on her side. To this day I keep wondering why suddenly men—educated, respectable men like myself—are not that credible anymore. I've no idea what women's lib has actually achieved. As far as I can see, it did a great job on our masculinity." Larry's voice had returned to its previous strength.

"You asked me what happened. I wish I knew. In front of my very eyes my wife changed from a friendly companion to a monster who used psychological jargon to push me out of her life. I was left behind, a powerless shell of a man. I only hope my experience is the exception, not the rule. Perhaps you can tell me." He took a deep breath.

THE WEST COAST CROWD

"The worst of all is that I can't even tell anyone this. We men have the hardest time sharing our feelings with other men. Thank you for listening." He looked up and was about to say more, but checked himself. I looked at my watch.

"Thank you," I said. "I've got to stop now, but I would like to continue, if you can spare some time for me soon. Thank you very much." Larry was disappointed. He had just gotten into the mood.

"Wait a minute here," he said. "I kept a whole chunk of time aside for you and now suddenly you're off? Maybe you don't like to hear about liberated women who ruin their marriages because of some crazy ideas they get into their heads all of a sudden." He sounded really angry. I gathered my things and got up.

"I understand your feelings," I told him. "I'm not here to pass judgments or take sides. I'm merely collecting data. When can we meet again?" This seemed to appease him.

"How about this evening?" he asked. "We could go for a ride along the coast and park the car and talk. That is, if you still object to going to a restaurant with me. Please, do say yes."

"All right, we'll meet this evening on one condition: we continue with the interview." I agreed to his suggestion partly because, despite my objective distance, I could not help feeling a bit sorry for the husband who found himself caught unprepared in an ideology that had taken the women in his culture by storm, in which individual relationships were not always considered. Besides, his part of the story was so different from that of his ex-wife, so far, that I thought I was really onto something in terms of my original hypothesis. Perhaps it was inevitable that the two former spouses would view the divorce differently. If we met that evening, Larry's story could be completed without interruption.

Larry picked me up at my place on time. As we left the town and turned onto the old highway skirting the Pacific, I felt more relaxed and optimistic about my research. I might just come up with something interesting to say about this very popular topic, I thought. Even Larry, in his well-groomed appearance, seemed less intimidating. He parked the car in a quiet area close to the water. The ocean was in low tide, making a soft *lap, lap* sound from a few tiny breakers here and there. The twilight was yet to come.

Larry took a blanket from the trunk and spread it on the sand. I took the tape-recorder out of my bag and sat down. "Please begin anywhere you wish," I said as I pressed the button.

He went on for over an hour, pouring out his disappointment, confusion, and anger over his ex-wife's behavior. He rarely mentioned anything to indicate that he might have had something to do with the situation. He talked a great deal about betrayal. He sounded sad, rather than merely angry this time. I had to change the tape twice.

As I listened to his story, I began to see that in a way I was offering him a service. It occurred to me later that he was using me—to unload the bitterness he hadn't had a chance to before this. Oh well, I thought, anthropologists use their informants and I am perhaps one of the few to reciprocate the service. I even felt a bit noble about it all.

Around eight p.m., I told him that I had enough information. We could stop and return. "Thank you for all the work. I need to transcribe these tapes now, before I lose the mood."

"Would you consider paying me for my work," he asked, "by accepting my invitation for dinner?"

"Thank you, but I really must get back." It was not hard to decline the invitation. I felt I had already paid for his service.

On the way back Larry was quiet for a while. Then suddenly, he pulled off the road and stopped the car.

"Tell me," he asked, "don't you find me attractive at all?" I began to stammer from the shock of the question. Without waiting for my answer, he turned and pulled me toward him, gripping my shoulders strongly. This time I reacted fast. I pulled myself away from him with such force that it took him by surprise. He let go of me and started the car again. I was stupefied for several minutes by the whole event, and got quite angry with myself that I had not done anything to prevent it and had not reacted to his advances with more vigor.

"So, should we say we'll meet on Saturday for dinner?" said Larry very casually when we reached my place, as if nothing had happened. "Or would you prefer lunch? I know a place..."

I opened the car door, searching my mind for something strong enough to say to put Mr. Informant in his place. What came out sounded very Californian and benign compared to what I felt.

THE WEST COAST CROWD

"Get lost!"

— 1971 —

In 1972 I received a doctorate in Psychological Anthropology—from a department that was Freudian in orientation. I wrote a dissertation from the material I had collected in 1967 on my own in West Bengal. It was on Bengali women. The University of Chicago Press accepted a revised version of the dissertation for publication as a book. I was then offered a teaching position in Denver at the University of Colorado. In my first year of teaching, however, I began to feel oppressed by the administrative policies of the academic system. Once again, as I had in my first fieldwork in the Khasi Hills, I faced a major professional crisis. The anthropology I was expected to teach twelve hours a week soon became lifeless for me. The people whom I had encountered in the field, who had enriched my life so profoundly, disappeared rapidly behind the academic anthropology. It felt hypocritical to teach young people things about which I could not be enthusiastic myself. I was desperate to escape. Around this time I stumbled one evening onto an essay written by the Swiss psychiatrist Carl Gustav Jung. I had not read Jung's work before. The essay, "Answer to Job," was like a breath of fresh air to me. Immediately, I knew I would have to explore the ideas of this new-found scholar. Two years later, in 1975, I went to Switzerland to study at the C.G. Jung Institute in Zurich. While studying there, it became clear to me that the objective work of psychology would have to be combined with the subjective experience of personal analysis. Six years of training and personal analysis led at last to a diploma in Analytical Psychology, certifying me to be a practicing analyst. Now I could work with individual human beings face to face, accompanying them on the journey of their fate—yet I remained highly aware of the cultural imperatives in their lives. This journey to Switzerland, which was also a journey to my unconscious psyche, inevitably brought the cultural, personal, and transpersonal dimensions of my life together. It was a painful as well as rewarding journey of self-discovery, which rendered my original concern about the individual and the culture less relevant and, should I say, transcended it. This shift, which was so important in my professional and emotional life, has, I believe, made me a different kind of observer of human nature and culture.

In The Land Of The Swiss

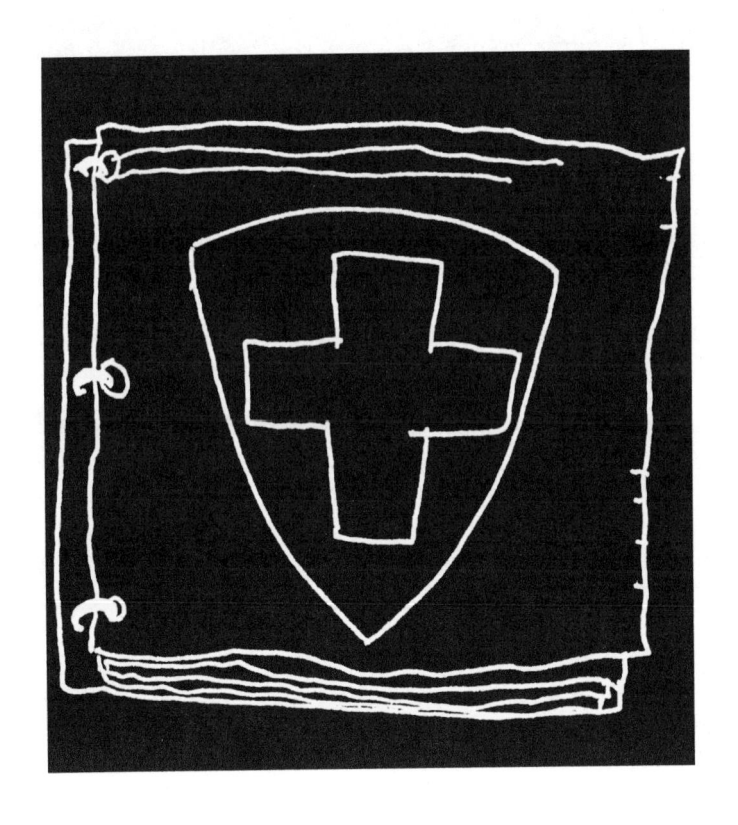

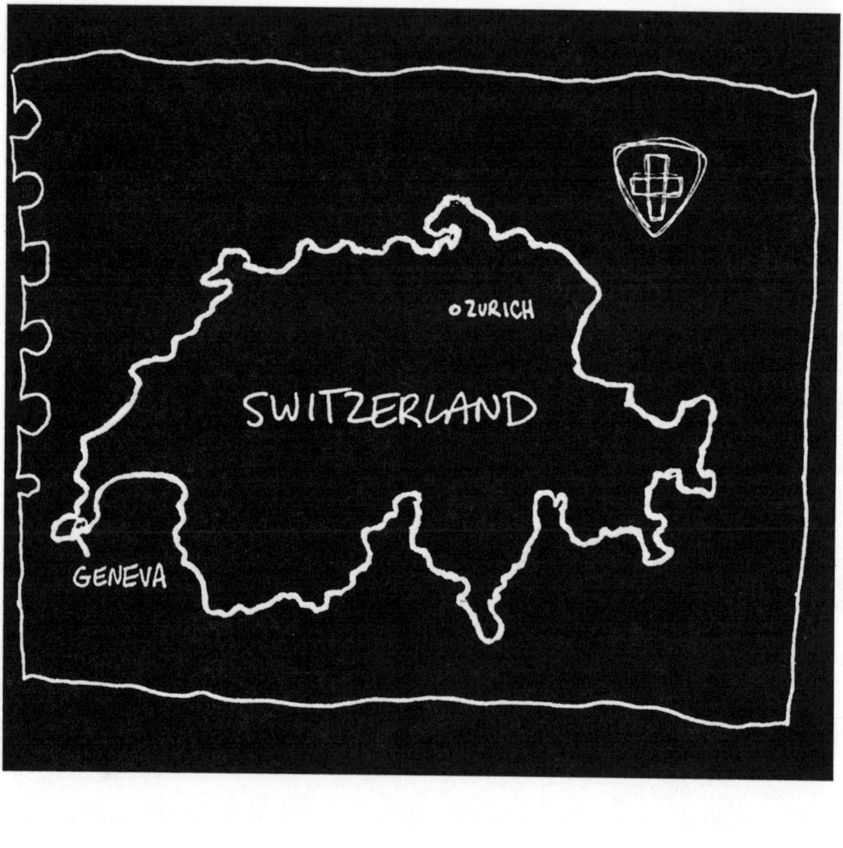
ZURICH
SWITZERLAND
GENEVA

Gossip and Legend

Within a few days of my arrival in Switzerland I was invited by a young Swiss couple to stay at their home until the start of my studies at the Jung Institute. The couple, Annamarie and Dieter, whom I had met in California a few years earlier, lived in a small town forty kilometers east of Zurich.

I accepted their kind invitation gladly. The peace of the small town would be a welcome respite before the demands of the Institute. Life among the quiet mountain meadows and calm streams would be better for my state of mind than the banks and shopping districts of Zurich. Indeed, the general atmosphere proved not only peaceful, but warm and protected as the valleys within the high ranges of the Alps.

In America, Annamarie had been employed by Swissair, and Dieter, an engineer, had been in on-the-job training. She stopped working when they were married. They had both traveled widely and were knowledgeable about cultures and people outside Switzerland.

The couple settled in Annamarie's ancestral village, where she had inherited a sturdy barn from her mother. Together they had renovated the barn into a cozy home. It had a large attic which served over the winter months as a nursery to seedlings and plants for their large garden. I noticed how scientific Dieter was in attending to the seedlings. Rows of small plastic pots stood under artificial lights even now, before the autumn was very far along.

Two floors below, in the kitchen, his wife was equally scientific about household gadgets, although she remained traditional in her cooking. I marveled at a tiny calculator that she took from her apron pocket when she did the household accounts after her twice-daily shopping trips. "I couldn't live without it," she said.

Yet I once saw her squeeze all the juice out of a cucumber before making a salad. "Why are you throwing all the vitamins away?" I asked.

"I suppose you're right," she said, unembarrassed. "But my mother taught me to do it this way, so that the salad remains crispy."

Among the many old customs observed by Annamarie and Dieter was one I truly admired. They kept in close touch with their relatives, some of whom occasionally joined us for meals. Annamarie's widowed father ate with us regularly.

Although I could not yet understand the local dialect—and knew, really, only minimal German—it was interesting to me to see and hear the family talk about matters that are universal. As a rule, most Swiss will not speak German unless they have to. I recalled the early stages of my fieldwork in societies where I had not known the language. By paying attention to body language and all the other nuances of non-verbal communication, I learned things which would likely be lost in a purely verbal exchange. I tried to tell Annamarie one day that language is used as often to conceal as to reveal. She apologized, once again, that her relatives could not speak English, or even German, well.

Watching Annamarie, I could not help comparing her with many American women of her age. She seemed to possess an extraordinary sense of herself. She did not give the impression of merely playing the role of a contented housewife—cooking, washing, ironing, gardening, and shopping twice a day for the meals: she *was* content. She had been exposed to the world. She had traveled and had been to college. Yet I saw her raise no questions about her role and duties in life. At this time, the mid-seventies, after I had witnessed the discontent among women in America, her behavior was indeed a phenomenon to me.

Elaborate meals were ready every day exactly at noon when Dieter came home. Annamarie's father, Herr Haefely, who lived one block away, would appear at the same time. The noon meal is the major one of the day in Swiss households, and the tradition continues because of the customary two-hour midday break throughout the country. In the evening, Annamarie would prepare a traditional apple pie, or a hot soup and salad with coffee and cake as dessert. Again, the four of us would gather at the

IN THE LAND OF THE SWISS

table to eat and talk. Sometimes a couple of cousins would drop in and share the meal.

They all began to accept me as Annamarie's and Dieter's friend, who came from America but was Indian. Within a few days, I began to feel quite at home, despite the language problem.

I compared my first entry into American culture with my current experience in Switzerland. The Americans had seemed more curious and eager to entertain. There, at various gatherings, I was asked many questions—some of which were rather ridiculous—such as had I ever met a Maharaja or seen a cobra in the streets of Calcutta. My American hosts were enthusiastic to make my first weeks in their country a success. Here, in this small town, people showed little interest openly, although I was sure they were aware of my existence. One afternoon, Annamarie and I took a leisurely walk through the town. She pointed out the houses of relatives and friends. More than once, I became aware of a pair of eyes peering from behind the lace curtains.

"Do you think they know about me?" I asked.

"I am sure they do," replied Annamarie, "although no one has asked me or Dieter directly about you. We Swiss are very careful about the privacy of others. Mind you, that does not mean we don't gossip among ourselves."

"Oh? What kind of gossip do you think these women behind the curtains are having about me?"

"I cannot say," said Annamarie, cautiously. "Perhaps they are just curious about how we met. After all, in this little town, not many people have seen an Indian woman in flesh and blood before." She smiled.

After this conversation, I was even more aware of the table talk at meals. In fact, I could decode some of the more heated gossip from the repetition of certain names and expressions. It was necessary, however, to ask Annamarie what exactly Frau Hunsicher had done.

Two weeks passed in this manner. Then, gradually, I discovered that though I was being offered warm hospitality, my boundaries as a guest were subtly drawn. I was, for example, not allowed to perform certain kinds of housework except in a marginal fashion. I would be intrusive, otherwise.

One morning as I was walking in the garden, I saw Annamarie carry a basket full of wash to the yard—and leave it quickly to answer the telephone. I did what I would have done anywhere else. I began to hang the wash on the neatly arranged clothes-lines. Since neither Annamarie nor Dieter would ever ask me to do anything around the house, I took this opportunity to help out a bit.

"Thank you, Manisha, for hanging the wash," said Annamarie when she returned. But she proceeded to remove it from the lines. "You see, you have mixed up all the colors. It's better to put all the greens together and separate them from the reds. Also, the socks should not be with the blouses." Her voice was gentle. She rearranged the wash with patience and dexterity. I realized then she was not joking.

"I am awfully sorry. I don't, didn't realize..." I could not say more. I did not know how to react. In all my encounters with different cultures, I could not recall having seen anyone rearrange the wash according to the colors or categories.

"You may think it's crazy to be so fussy," she continued, hanging the clothes as she spoke. "In America, I have seen, nobody cares about how things are organized or how they look. Actually it's quite convenient to arrange the wash this way. It's easier to fold them when they are dry."

"Now that you explain, I guess it makes sense," I offered, partly to hide my amazement. I could not yet grasp why folding the dry wash was easier when it had been hung according to its color.

"Besides," added Annamarie, "my mother, grandmother and all their ancestors did it this way. I like to keep some of the old customs. I feel good following them.".

"That's very nice, Annamarie. I have all the respect for people who practice age-old customs. As you know I, too, come from an old culture." I caught myself, having said something that sounded superfluous.

After this episode, I avoided areas where mistakes were less predictable, therefore inevitable. Consequently my curiosity and sense of adventure in discovering a new culture were curbed for a while. I began to pay more attention to their rules. I came to realize that despite all my social skills and anthropological training, I still did not always know how to be a gracious guest and a

IN THE LAND OF THE SWISS

participant observer at the same time. I was in Switzerland, the land of the original puritans. The rules were not only different, but must be followed with due respect.

Again, I tried to keep myself amused with all the table talk. While the selectman, Herr Schmidt, was abusing his power by bringing in his brother-in-law onto the town council, Frau Hunsicher was flouting tradition by having a clandestine affair with a young working-class Italian. I could not be sure if it were the adultery or the choice of lover that was more condemned. The women seemed less forgiving about the act, while the men were really upset that the young man was Italian. Annamarie's father, Herr Haefely, seemed interested only in the town council scandal. He shook his head again and again in disbelief over the nepotism.

This law-abiding citizen seemed very excited one afternoon, arguing with his son-in-law over something. They spoke so fast that I could not catch a single word. Afterwards, Annamarie explained that her father objected to a new bill in the legislature which would reduce the work week of a Swiss government employee from forty to thirty-six hours. Dieter had tried to play the devil's advocate, arguing that if the bill passed they all could benefit from the extra leisure-time. But the old man would not hear of it. Later, I found out that the bill was defeated by a landslide majority vote, so deeply held is the work ethic by the people of this land of Calvin[32].

On a Sunday morning, Annamarie told me that they had to go to Graubunden to attend a family funeral. "It's for a granduncle of Dieter's on his father's side. I never knew him well. But it's family, so I have to attend. May I ask you a favor, Manisha?"

"Of course."

"Would you mind terribly, keeping my father company over supper? I have already prepared the soup and pie for both of you."

"Sure," I responded, still eager for a chance to help out. "I'll be happy to warm up the soup and serve us. I may even try a few words of the dialect with your dad."

---

[32] John Calvin (1509–1564), born Jean Cauvin in France, was a theologian and religious leader who studied in Basel and later made Geneva a center for the Protestant Reformation.

"Thanks. We'll be back tomorrow, as soon as we can."

"Don't worry about anything. Have a safe trip." I welcomed this change of routine. Eating supper with Herr Haefely, who spoke not a word of English *or* German, would be a challenge.

Herr Haefely arrived on time. As he entered he smiled and touched his cap to greet me. We both said "Greutsis"[33] and sat down to eat. I had already laid the table and warmed the soup and bread. The old man sat across the table. He removed his cap and put it on an empty chair. For the first time I noticed that he had a full head of dark hair. He cannot be that old after all, I thought. I felt sorry that he had lost his wife already. I wondered how she had died.

We passed the salt and bread to each other. He cut the pie and I poured the coffee. When the supper was over, he stacked the dishes next to the kitchen sink and I shook the crumbs off the tablecloth. Later he stood near me, drying the dishes as I washed them. He put them away, exactly where they belonged. I was grateful because I had forgotten.

All through this, however, I had the distinct feeling that Herr Haefely was staring at me with veiled curiosity. His eyes kept moving over a particular part of my upper torso. Yet I could not call it a lascivious look. Even when he said good night and left, and I turned off the dining-room lights, I was not sure I had interpreted his stares correctly.

In these weeks I had lived with his daughter's family, I had had no inkling that he could be "the type." On the other hand, how could I dismiss the roving eyes of that evening? Had he waited to be alone with me? I decided to let my suspicions rest until I had further evidence. Besides, I would be off to Zurich in a few days. There was no point in stirring up anything now.

Next day, Annamarie and Dieter returned. We had the usual lunch with her father. But now it happened again. The old man was staring at me in that same way as often as he could. This continued for another three days. He attempted no moves, only stares. Any other action would have betrayed what he really meant. I could not quite shake off my discomfort every time I met him. I wore very loose farmer's blouses—to defend against his penetrating eyes.

---

[33] The usual "Greetings."

Before leaving, I invited Annamarie and Dieter out for dinner. It was a way to thank them for their hospitality during my first month in a new country. Half way through the meal, after a few glasses of delicious Swiss wine, I felt brave enough to broach the subject that was on my mind. I began by mentioning something about older people and their loneliness after the death of a spouse.

"By the way, Annamarie," I said, "how long has your father been widowed? He does not look that old. It must be hard. Fortunately, you two live so close and he can be part of your family."

"Oh, he is eagerly waiting for his grandchildren to arrive," said Dieter, looking at his wife affectionately. "As soon as Anna is ready we'll have a family. Not just to please the grandpa, of course."

"Why are you asking about my father?" asked Annamarie. "Has he said something to you about being lonely? You must understand the dialect quite well now."

"Yes, why?" said Dieter. "Has the old man shown some special interest in you? I keep telling Anna..." A look from his wife made him stop in the middle of his opinion.

"No, no," I said, cautiously. "He hasn't said anything. It's something else. I don't know how to describe this. And, I may be totally wrong." I then told them about my observations, as gently and as diplomatically as I could, with several "ifs" and "maybes." Annamarie was quiet for a long time.

"I'm very surprised to hear this," she said at last. "My father has never shown any interest in my women friends. With you, he was very curious from the beginning because you come from India. He asked me a few questions, but I could never guess it might be..." She was silent again.

"I am awfully sorry and terribly embarrassed," she continued, after a while. "Please, give me a little time. I can ask him directly. We have been fairly close since my mother's death." Dieter kept looking back and forth at Annamarie and me, appearing a bit incredulous. But as we were leaving the restaurant, he whispered something to me.

"Anna forgets that her father is a man too. Poor devil."

IN THE LAND OF THE SWISS

I left the next day for Zurich, hugging Annamarie, kissing Dieter on both cheeks, and shaking hands with others in the family, including Herr Haefely.

A week later, Annamarie called to meet me for tea at one of the cafes in the main railway station. She was coming to Zurich for the day. It was nice to see her and to know that she held nothing against me for the news that evening about her father.

"I've really missed you and your home," I said, once we had found a table, "especially the clean bed warmed by the Swiss Army hot water bottle."

"You can come back to enjoy all that anytime you wish," she said. "By the way, you need not worry about a dirty old man anymore. This is what my father said to me when I asked him for an explanation: 'Remember Uncle Johannes, your grandmother's next-door neighbor, who collects old books and reads them? You used to borrow children's books from him. You loved to tell your mother and me those stories, do you remember?' 'Of course,' I said, 'I loved those books with pictures and strange stories from China, Japan, and all those distant lands.' 'Well,' my father said, 'Johannes once told me that he had read a very interesting old German book of legends from all over the world. In that book there was a section devoted to stories from India. Strange things happen in India. According to one story, women there have *three breasts* instead of two. So, when you told me that you'd have a guest—a woman from India—I was curious to see if that story were true or not. But, after looking closely, I still cannot be sure. Would you do me a favor and ask your friend if this is really true?' 'If that old book said so then perhaps it was true in some ancient time. Let me ask Manisha,' I said, not really knowing what to say."

Upon hearing the story I laughed. Annamarie joined me. We laughed so loud that other people in the cafe looked at us. I ran out of breath.

"So what are you going to tell your father?" I asked.

"I think I shall tell him that Manisha won't tell me because it's a secret and no Indian woman can share it with anyone"

"That's perfect. You are good, Annamarie." We had another good laugh, and left the cafe. Though we talked on the phone occasionally, she had never mentioned the subject again.[34]

* * *

The next year I was at a country fair in Frascati, near Rome. It was a harvest festival, with country-style ham and bread being consumed in great quantities. Fruity Frascati wine ran like water and the Italians ate, drank, and talked all at the same time. At a stall where freshly baked bread of various sizes and shapes was being sold, I noticed a few bread dolls hanging from the canvas wall. The dolls were chubby ladies with three breasts. A small tag announced their name—*Miss Poppea*.

"Do you know anything about the origin of these three-breasted dolls?" I asked my Italian companion. "Any story behind them?"

"Well, not really," he said. "But I think they may be a folk version of Ceres, the ancient Roman goddess of fertility. I have seen pictures of Ceres with many breasts to indicate her powers of fertility and nurturance."

My companion looked amused when I turned to buy one.

— *1976–1977* —

---

[34] A few years later, as I was preparing a lecture on Hindu goddesses, I stumbled on the following myth from South India:

Goddess Minakshi was born of a king who had wanted a son and treated her like a son. As she came of age she developed three breasts, one of which disappeared when she met her husband Shiva.

I wrote a letter to Annamarie, telling her of the myth:

"Obviously, the goddesses in India can have more than two breasts, which can then become two. We mortals don't have such privileges. I owe your father this information. You and I no longer need to be secretive about the goddess' breasts."

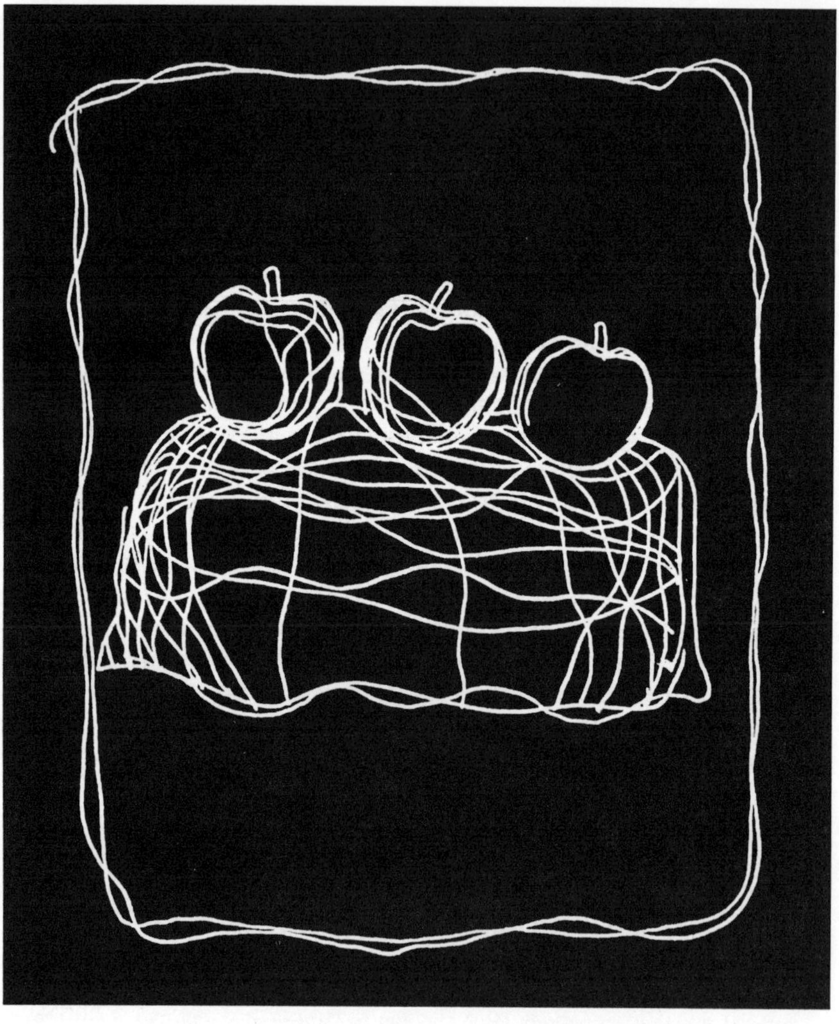

Swiss Encounters

It was a rainy September morning in 1975 when I first arrived in Switzerland to study at the C.G. Jung Institute. Within minutes of landing, I had occasion to observe how quiet and orderly was the Zurich airport. The continuous cold drizzle from the grey sky outside added to the atmosphere of soundlessness. Even the friends and relatives who awaited the arriving passengers were standing beyond a soundproof glass wall.

The bus-ride into the city confirmed this feeling, except where the Italian construction workers were digging up the streets with their powerful drills. I could escape the sound and sight of excavation only by looking out intently at the buildings and roadside objects. I soon realized that there were more banks than chocolate shops on any given street in this city.

A month later, it was time to begin my studies in earnest. I was pleased to find a small attic room not far from the Institute. The rent was within my budget, although I had to share the unheated bathroom and shower. The landlady cleaned the rooms regularly, changing the linens every week for freshly ironed ones. I liked this austere living. It reminded me of my college days. I kept meticulous account of all my expenses and was proud that I was rapidly surpassing even the Swiss in handling my money with such frugality and care.

In Switzerland all bills, including taxes, are paid in cash at the beginning of every month, through the post office. There I would see long lines of people, mostly women, who paid their bills and quickly moved to another long line, ready with their passbooks to deposit their monthly savings.

One morning I went to the post office to pay my bills and to send a birthday parcel to a friend in America. I was in a hurry because I had to keep an important appointment within the hour. There was a long line. By the time I paid my bills and had moved to another window to weigh the parcel and to the next to buy stamps, I had barely enough time to keep the appointment. To make matters worse, I had very little change. While the line behind me grew longer, I gave the clerk a hundred-franc bill.

Despite the fast service, I felt impatient waiting. As I pasted the stamps on the parcel, the woman behind the window took out several bills of small denomination and a stack of coins and pushed them neatly across the counter. Quickly, I gathered everything and shoved it all inside my handbag and moved out of the line. I was at the door when I heard a loud and angry voice. I looked back and saw the clerk gesticulating at me from behind the window. In my limited understanding of the Swiss dialect, I could not tell what she was trying to say. The few words we had exchanged earlier were in German. She was too angry now to bother with her second language and kept pointing at my handbag. I became nervous. Had she seen me licking the stamps instead of using the glue on the counter? But, that was impossible—she herself had licked the pages of a book of stamps only moments before I reached her window. The longer I pondered, the angrier she became. Then I understood. She must have returned too much money. I went to the window again and took out all the bills and change she had given me, spreading them out on the counter within her reach. I was very anxious about the time. Her face relaxed. She took each bill in her palm, one at a time, smoothing it gently, then folding it, once in the middle, then again lengthwise. She folded two ten-franc bills, and three of twenty-francs. She put them together and held them between her index and middle fingers, then with her other hand, stacked the coins according to their size and value. She pushed the coins and the neatly folded bills gently toward me.

The whole operation could not have taken more than a minute. It felt like an hour. She looked relaxed and calm now. It took me a moment to register the meaning of the event. Without even thinking about the time and place, I began to scream in plain English.

"How *dare* you fold and arrange my money?" By now the whole line was quite interested. A screaming foreigner in a neighborhood post office is not a common occurrence in this country. The last thing I remember before rushing out was the bewildered face at the window.

IN THE LAND OF THE SWISS

I was fifteen minutes late for my appointment already. I ran for the streetcar. Once inside, I sat by a window and cooled off. The streetcar made a turn, passing the main branch of the largest bank in Switzerland. The building was magnificent: an impressive facade of tall marble columns and elegantly decorated windows. I had a revelation. I began to understand the event at the post office.

I had treated money with disrespect. The clerk was merely teaching me to show veneration to something sacred to their culture. How could I miss all the rituals around money in this country? The best quality paper, the best printing, the symbols and images selected through a nation-wide competition among the best artists—and the way every Swiss handles the bills and coins? As an anthropologist I should have known better.

Meanwhile, from my studies and my personal analysis, it was becoming clear that the things which annoy us most are often our own unconscious tendencies. The idea was novel and, at the same time, hard to accept. But one day I caught myself folding an American dollar exactly the way the clerk had done in the Zurich post office. The dollar did not have the same crisp feel to it, however. I have to admit that I am a bit like the Swiss, I thought, perhaps in more ways than one. Or, perhaps I am on the way toward integrating some of my annoying unconscious habits.

In my stumbling adaptation to the Swiss culture, which is heavily influenced by strict puritanical morality, I encountered such virtues as honesty and a high regard for the privacy of others. Both these qualities, I argued with myself, must contribute to the admirable efficiency in running everyday life in this country.

In the basement of the house where I lived, the tenants were each assigned separate times for doing wash and separate lines for drying it. If by chance one load did not dry by the assigned hour, the next tenant would put the damp clothes in a neat pile, following the rule to the letter. One rainy day my damp wash was piled up this way. Annoyed, I tried to explain to my successor that we could perhaps share the lines this time. She did not understand how one could break the rule.

A similar event took place one Saturday afternoon. I had almost forgotten to stock up on food for the weekend. In Switzerland, all grocery stores are closed from four p.m. Saturday till two p.m. Monday. It was ten minutes to four. I rushed to the nearest grocery. The front door was not yet locked, but I was stopped from entering. Only the shoppers inside were allowed to use the door—as an exit. I begged to be let in to pick up some eggs, bread, and milk, which I could have done in less than ten minutes. The uniformed doorkeeper shook his head vigorously, saying, "Nein, nein, nein!" I realized then that honesty and discipline do not necessarily come with mercy. That weekend I lived on four very expensive eggs which I bought from a restaurant-owner—a Brazilian—who easily broke the rule of selling uncooked food. The whole incident was hard to rationalize, given my angry feelings toward the system. I tried to argue with myself that an individual's convenience must be sacrificed for the smooth running of a society.

In my personal analysis, I was wrestling with conflicting issues of personal and social ethics. My well-meaning intentions to appreciate a law-abiding, rule-following nation were not enough. Something inside me rose in anger—from impotency against the power of a system that has little room for unpredictability and irrationality. Could acceptance of the Swiss world-view, I wondered, help me in my own life?...

One cold January morning I was waiting for a bus to the main train station. I had a small suitcase. The Limmat River, which splits the city in two, was quiet and dark on my left. On my right rose the terrace-like hills of Zurichberg. Before me, the high steeple of the medieval cathedral, the Grossmuenster, pierced the clear sky. It was so cold that hardly anyone was out. A chilly wind blew into my bones despite my heavy coat, hat, and scarf.

The bus was not due for another twelve minutes. I looked around for shelter. About fifty yards away stood a kiosk with an overhead electric heater. Leaving the suitcase at the bus-stop, I walked to the kiosk. I kept an eye out for the approaching bus and another on the suitcase. A minute later an elderly couple passed by with two bags of groceries. They had gone only a few yards beyond the bus-stop when they turned and retraced their steps. They came up to my suitcase, stopped, looked around, and put down their bags.

Curious to see what would happen next, I watched them without moving or saying anything. The man now examined the bag carefully and spotted the hanging tag. He tried to read it, stopping to look for something in his pockets. His wife opened her handbag and took out a pair of glasses and gave them to him. When he was reading the tag, she turned toward the kiosk and walked to where I stood. She asked the kiosk attendant for paper and pencil. She walked back to the bus-stop and copied my name and address from the tag.

Although I was still curious to see what they would do next to ensure the safety of a stranger's bag, it felt cruel to wait any longer. Besides, the bus would arrive in a minute. I walked up to the couple and told them in German that the suitcase belonged to me. I thanked them many times for their concern.

The man looked at me suspiciously and asked for proof of my identity. To my surprise, he began to lecture me, in a dialect I could not follow. It could have been about my carelessness toward my possessions, or about my dishonesty in claiming someone else's bag as my own. Whatever it was, I was not about to oblige him by producing my passport. The timely arrival of the bus saved the day. I forgot my admiration of a moment before toward their honesty and sense of responsibility. As I jumped inside the electric door of the bus, dragging my suitcase with me, I left behind two solidly shocked citizens.

For weeks after that, I was nervous every time I went to the mailbox. The elderly couple had my name and address. Knowing the Swiss regard for efficiency, I was sure the police would track me down for verification or whatever. The official letter never arrived. I regained my original trust in the reasonableness of all human beings, the Swiss included.

Not long after the incident at the bus-stop, a friend came from America for a visit. It was a welcome change for me. I needed a break from the city, and from the heavy routine of classes and analysis....

I had been in Switzerland well over a year by then. In my personal analysis, the unforeseen encounters with my unconscious were not always easy to deal with. The figures and images of my dream-life brought home the unpalatable fact that I too had a darkness within my psyche which was hard to acknowledge consciously. In addition, the adjustments to a culture so alien to that of my upbringing had taken a toll. In the past, when I visited a country for the purposes of fieldwork or study, my encounters with strangers were not as complicated as those here in Switzerland. I had been able, somehow, to keep my distance.

I did not realize how exhausted I had become. But seeing me after more than a year, Mark, my friend, noticed it immediately.

"How are you?" he asked solicitously. "You look quite tired. Have you been taking care of yourself?"

"Well, it hasn't been easy," I replied, almost vacantly. "Analysis is exciting, but hard. Encountering one's own shadow has its pain." I looked at him, and became more focused. "I hadn't the foggiest idea of my own darkness. The more I am analyzed and face this painful realization, the less complacent I become. Also, I cannot *project out* everything I dislike. It's hard but, at the same time, deeply satisfying. Do you know what I'm saying?"

"No, I don't," he said. "But from the look of it, you need a break from all this magnificent misery."

"I've been so busy and careful with money so far that I haven't allowed myself even to think about a holiday."

"We can rectify that right away," Mark declared. "Can you get away for a while? You can show me the sights of Switzerland. I'll drive. And I shall make sure you have fun. No demons to encounter, except yours truly." I could not help laughing.

"That sounds good to me. At least—for a weekend. You're right. I need a break. Desperately."

We packed a few things, rented a car and, the next morning, a Sunday, started off to the south—toward the beautiful slopes of the Rossberg[35]. The idea of a weekend in the rarefied mountain air made me feel better already.

The morning was crisp and clear, with the bright sun in front of us. Although it was early spring, there was not a single rain cloud in the sky. The warmth of the sun was strong enough to overcome the musty smell of the season. But soon it became clear that the day was in the grip of the foehn, that warm yet unwelcome wind from the heart of the African desert.

"You can see the effect of the foehn[36] on the drivers," I said to Mark. "Everyone drives faster than usual. There is a sense of

---

[35] The Rossberg is a three-mile long mountain ridge south of Zürich, rising less than a mile above sea-level.
[36] Technically, a foehn is any warm, dry, gusty wind that periodically descends the leeward slope of a mountain or mountain range. In the Alps, the wind from Africa pushes moist air up the windward slope,

euphoria in the air, which can lead to accidents and disasters. It's a mixed blessing, this foehn."

"How so?"

"Well, initially, you get a feeling of well-being from the warm temperature. Everything appears sharp and clear. See how close the Alps look? But the same wind also brings headaches and nausea. The number of highway accidents rises and the stock market drops. And in the hospitals, all major surgery is postponed. Everything, including machines, behaves crazily."

"Interesting. So, you could say that the foehn is actually Mother Nature's way of interfering with the air-tight Swiss efficiency. How ingenious of her."

"That's right," I said. "I hadn't thought of it that way. You're absolutely right." I felt pleased by this anomaly, something I had not noticed myself until then. I began to feel more light-hearted. "Let's hope," I continued, "that we'll be in the mountains before the foehn has any effect on *us*. Let me know if you feel anything unusual. I haven't felt its effect myself yet. Maybe the foehn leaves foreigners alone."

"I feel okay, so far," he said. "It would be fun to see how this wind effects an American. Oops, I think we missed our exit."

We took the next exit, for what we thought was another road to the mountains. Within minutes we entered the town of Einsiedeln.

"I'm sorry," said Mark. "It must be the foehn." We laughed at the turn of events.

"Isn't it just like the Swiss?" he mused. "Even their wind is so damn efficient. It really disorients you."

"Look," I said with enthusiasm, "since we are already here, why don't we explore the town?"

A little reluctantly, he turned toward the center of town. Before long, we saw hundreds of people, all walking in one direction. We followed slowly for a while, then parked the car and walked awhile with the crowd. I asked a woman where everyone was going. She pointed ahead to the dome of a cathedral and walked on pensively.

---

where the increasing water vapor turns to precipitation. Then, the now dry air descends the leeward slope, warming as it goes.

"Let's see what's up," I said. By the time we arrived at the plaza in front of the cathedral, it had occurred to me that it must be Easter Sunday. I felt drawn to stay with the crowd. I told my companion to come back in an hour for me.

"Okay," he said, looking slightly disappointed. "I will find a cafe somewhere and study the map for a detour to the mountains. Are you sure you need to spend a whole hour? You're not even Christian."

"I'm sure. Please." I went on alone.

I tried to go into the cathedral, but it was overflowing. I looked for a gap through which to squeeze. It was impossible. Still, the sounds and smells of High Mass reached me. I saw several old women, their heads covered, kneel on the threshold.

It dawned on me that Einsiedeln[37] was famous for its cathedral, a masterpiece of the Baroque, and that the cathedral was famous for its statue of a Black Madonna. Although I had always been interested in the beauty of churches and cathedrals, this time it was different. I seemed to have no choice but to participate in the Easter Mass at Einsiedeln. Waves of inexplicable emotion began to lift me from the surrounding chaos. I stood in a daze.

Then, the service came to an end. A huge flow of people began to leave the nave. I stepped aside to let them pass; the wait seemed interminable. Then I hurried inside. Hardly anyone was there, except a few acolytes putting things in order. They were too busy to notice me.

I walked slowly toward the life-size wooden image of the Madonna. She stood with baby Jesus in her arm. Her dark face was serene and compassionate. I closed my eyes and bowed down to touch my forehead to the floor, Indian style, in veneration. Tears came over me. I sat there a long time, shedding many tears, the only offering I could make to this renowned goddess of healing. A nun came to ask if she could help. They were about to close the cathedral for the afternoon. I went outside.

In the bright sun, it took me a while before I saw Mark waving from an outdoor cafe across the plaza. When we met he

---

[37] A town in the Swiss canton of Schwyz. A Benedictine monastery was founded here in the 10th century, the Madonna was installed in the 14th century, and the great Abbey was built in the 18th.

looked at me for a few seconds, but refrained from speaking. He went to get the car. In the car I suggested we go back to Zurich. I was not in the mood to go to the mountains. I said little. I could not tell him that I had just undergone the most profound experience of my life.

I had had no idea how much I needed those moments in the cathedral. No wonder, I thought, that thousands of pilgrims from all over Europe come to attend the Easter Service in the Black Madonna's temple each year.

"You didn't tell me that the foehn can also bring about miracles," said my companion, trying to lighten the atmosphere.

"Maybe it was not the foehn," I said, "but the Madonna, that made you miss the exit. She is famous for her healing power—healing tired and heavy souls."

— 1976–1978 —

The next two stories take place after a sojourn back to America—and after my remarriage. By now I was deeply into my training to become a Jungian psychotherapist. I was also teaching as a visiting professor at Zurich University and had begun to feel more settled. As time went, I understood and appreciated the Swiss culture and psychology better. I could see, for example, the psychological compensation of the seasonal carnivals—which break all rules and norms—to the orderly perfectionism of the Swiss consciousness. After watching the ominous Basel Fassnacht, a winter carnival with bizarre masks and music in the bone-chilling hours before dawn, I could see what C. G. Jung had really meant by the forces of the collective unconscious. The more I delved into his ideas and the more I experienced analysis of my own unconscious, the less problematic became the dichotomy between the object and subject, profession and emotion. Strangers and their cultures ceased to be causes of struggles in adaptation. They became steps toward self-realization.

The Neighborly Frau Buechli

In 1979 my husband and I moved to Brugg, a small town in northwest Switzerland, not far from the Black Forest. Our new home was one of fifteen apartments in a building perhaps a decade old. The building had an elevator, a parking garage, and a little courtyard—all shared in common by the tenants.

We had come from America, where we lived in a succession of places and it had always been easy to meet our new neighbors. Once, in a welcoming gesture, someone brought a cake. Another time, in a small town in New England, one family held an informal "coffee" to introduce us all around. But in general, a couple would simply stop by and put out their hands and start talking.

"Hello! We're Mary and Brian Chandler, your neighbors on the north," they might say. "Welcome to the neighborhood! Don't hesitate to ask if there's anything we can do. Just yell across the fence!"

In Brugg, however, after two weeks, no one had made the gesture. We decided to make one ourselves.

It was a Saturday when about six couples were invited to an open house between five and eight in the evening. This way the guests could come and go as they pleased. I had prepared some finger-food: some cold, some warm. My husband had bought a few bottles of good wine and local beer. I also had provision for tea and coffee, in case that's what some would like.

The doorbell rang exactly at five. A group of women and men were crowded together in the hallway in front of the elevator. How on earth, I wondered, could they all have come at the same time? When everyone was settled it occurred to me that perhaps they had planned to come together, because it would make everyone more at ease. After elaborate introductions we began to pass the food around.

One particular guest, Frau Buechli, appeared to be more outgoing and helpful. She took charge and mediated. Her English was far better than the others'. Everyone seemed eager to taste things. After devouring several samosas, one man said something in the dialect to his wife and looked briefly at me. "Gut, sehr gut," he said.

"Danke," I said. "Das ist samosa, ein Indische imbiss. Es freue mich das Sie es gut finden. Danke sehr." In my enthusiasm to try German I may have overdone it a bit.

The man looked at me with a blank stare, as if he understood not one word of what I said. His wife, in the meantime, took one samosa, bit into it, and dropped the rest on the floor—inadvertently, I presumed. She nudged her husband, who got her a glass of water.

"Sehr heiss fur mich," *It's too hot for me*, was her only comment.

"Wunderbar! Sie haben Deutsch sehr gut gelernt." This compliment came from Frau Buechli, when she saw my expression. She spoke German for the benefit of the others, I supposed. "Richtig?" she added, looking at the other guests, who did not bother even to nod.

At some point I began to wonder why no one had left, even though most of them had barely participated. Perhaps they have never heard of the concept "open house," I thought. They must have plans to leave together. Then I noticed that we had run out of all the food and drink. I signaled my husband to follow me to the kitchen.

"It's almost *nine*," I whispered. "No one looks ready to leave. There's no more food. What should we do?"

"Well, I really don't know how to make our guests leave," he said, half in jest. "This must be the first time we faced this particular predicament."

As we were debating what to do next, Frau Buechli put her head into the kitchen. "May I help with anything?" she asked.

"Yes," I said, "but we don't know how to put it." Embarrassed, I explained the problem and asked if she could help to solve it.

"Oh, I see," she said. "That's right. You did say open house. Now I remember hearing the expression in my English language class. Don't worry about the food. We all had enough. Let me see what I can do." She went back to the living room and said something to the others in the dialect. As she spoke, she picked up her handbag as if she were ready to leave. Miraculously, everyone stood up and gathered their belongings. They thanked us and bid good night.

"Danke Schoen."
"Danke Ihnen."
"Auf wiedersehen."
"Auf wiedersehen."

The group departed and we breathed a sigh of relief to be alone at last. Now we could prepare our dinner. Playing hosts did not allow us much opportunity to eat. But within ten minutes the doorbell rang again. It was Frau Buechli.

"May I come in?" she asked. "It was a wonderful party. I came back to see if you need any help with the clean-up." She was all smiles. I looked in desperation to my husband, wondering where the well-known Swiss sense of privacy had gone.

"Thank you for your thoughtfulness," he offered. "But it's all taken care of."

"We are about to get our dinner ready," I said, eager to proceed. "Would you care to join us?"

"Sure, if it's no trouble. I'll just call my son to tell him I'm here." Without any hesitation, Frau Buechli went to the telephone. I went to the kitchen, angry with myself for inviting a guest for dinner. I had no idea what to serve her. We ourselves could make do with toast and eggs. I could not possibly serve that to a guest at this hour, I thought. But why not?—she barged in on us after a long evening of snacks. I took two more eggs from the fridge.

"It really was a great party," said Frau Buechli, coming into the kitchen. "We here don't do things like that. Oh, you are making omelets. Why don't you add some *aromat*? Do you have any? I can go and get some from my kitchen. It will take only a few minutes."

"*Aromat*? Thank you, but I don't think it's necessary, whatever it is. Look, it's getting late. We are all quite tired. Let's just have our omelets and toast. Maybe another time you can tell me what it is." I began to carry the food to the dining table. She stepped up and took the things from my hands, then deftly laid them on the table.

"Herr professor, dinner is served," she said. I was astounded by her capacity to take over. My fatigue from the long evening was turning slowly into anger. It could also have been hypoglycemia.

"Please call me Anna," she said, smiling. "I have learned in my English class that in America it is the custom to use one's Christian name. And I would like to do the same, if you like."

"Of course. Why not?" said my husband, looking at me.

"Sure," I said. I just wanted this long evening of neighborliness to end.

As soon as we finished eating, Anna jumped up and gathered the dishes together. "I shall take care of these. Please get yourselves ready for bed. You worked very hard to give the party."

We did not have the energy to protest. We sat on the living room sofa with our feet up while our helpful neighbor washed and dried the dishes in the kitchen. Strangely, we felt resigned enough not to feel any discomfort.

After a while, I went into the kitchen to thank her. She had just opened the drawer to put in the dried forks and spoons. She looked shocked.

"Oh, no. Your spoons and knives are all mixed up. Let me fix them for you." Before I even understood what she meant, she had taken the whole drawer out and emptied its contents on the counter. She then proceeded to rearrange everything, I presumed, according to its category.

"Oh—*no*," I said. "There's no need to fix anything for me. Thank you for all your help. Please leave my forks and spoons alone."

"Okay. I see," she stammered. Her face registered more surprise and confusion than insult. "Well, good night then." She wiped her hands with the dish towel, went to the living room, said goodnight to my husband, and left.

That night in bed I pushed aside the guilt I felt for having been so rude to such a helpful neighbor. "Are you asleep?" I said to my husband. "What do you think? Is she just different and lacks a sense of proportion? Have I been unduly rude?"

"What? Who?" He sounded half awake. I wished I could fall asleep so easily. Perhaps I was overtired. Something about Frau Buechli reminded me of some of my California acquaintances. But I was not sure quite how.

A few weeks passed. We did not hear anything from Anna Buechli. I wondered if she was really hurt by my behavior the evening of the party. Meanwhile, I ran into some of the neighbors. Not one of them showed any recognition beyond the usual "Greutzis." Obviously we had not made any dent in the Swiss reserve, although at the party they had all said how happy they were to know us.

One afternoon when I came home from a walk, I saw a small package in front of the door. It contained a jar of spice with the word *Aromat* written on it, and was accompanied by a note from Anna Buechli. Relieved that I had not offended her too much, I telephoned her.

"Hello, Anna? This is Manisha. Thank you so much for the *aromat*. How have you been?"

"You are very welcome," she said. "You can use it in many things—salads, soups, omelets, anything you like... I have been very well, thank you. By the way, would you be home this evening? I'd like to drop in for a visit, if you don't mind."

"Just a minute, please. Let me ask my husband if he has anything planned," I said, and covered the receiver. My husband, who had been within earshot, signaled "no."

"You can meet her," he added. "I have to go out for a while anyway."

"Anna," I said, returning to the call, "my husband tells me that he needs to do some paperwork and he'd welcome some peace and quiet here. Why don't I drop in at your place instead?"

"Sure," said Anna. "Give me a couple of hours. I'll prepare Hans's supper first. We can meet after supper, then?"

"Fine. I'll come by later. Thanks." I hung up, unable to shake off my surprise at her quick manipulation of the time to her own advantage.

Immediately I regretted having agreed to her suggestion. In an hour I called her to say that I was too tired to do anything that evening. Perhaps we could meet another time. It felt good to be the manipulator this time.

"Okay," she said, sounding disappointed. "If you are free, let's have coffee tomorrow afternoon. Is four o'clock convenient for you?"

"Yes, four is fine. Thank you." I was trying to tell if she had picked up on my intentions. As on the night of the party, I began to feel guilty for all these assumptions I was making about her. Maybe she is one of those people who just takes things as they come, I thought. Nothing more than that. With this new possibility, I let Anna drop from my thoughts.

Next day I arrived at her door precisely at four, Swiss-style. Anna was all smiles as she took the small coffee-cake I had brought.

"Thank you, thank you very much. But it's very funny. Do you know that I have bought the same cake?" She laughed hard and led me by the hand to the dining table to show the cake, an exact replica of mine.

"It's from the Migro bakery," I said, laughing also.

"Thank God for Migro's!" she said, as we settled down to our coffee and cake. "Which one should I cut first? Do you think yours may be sweeter?" She winked like an American as she proceeded to cut the cake I had brought.

That evening Anna Beuchli and I had a long chat about many things. I learned a lot about her life. She had been married for ten years when her husband wanted a divorce. She was left with Hans, then seven years old and developing severe asthma. When Hans was in middle school, Anna went back to school herself to learn English and secretarial skills. Although she had enough alimony and child support she wanted to be independent. It took her another ten years to feel good about herself.

"My English teacher had lived in New York for many years," she said. "He helped me to see that I really was not a typical Swiss. I never was, you know. Since childhood I have always felt like a misfit in this country. That's why I seek out foreigners whenever I can. It's not everyday that people like you and your husband come to live in this small town. I hope you will forgive my eagerness to be with you." She stopped, and poured more coffee for both of us.

"Oh Anna, that's perfectly all right," I said, warming to her. "I have to admit, you took us by surprise. The Swiss we have met so far gave us a different impression. So I wasn't aware. Please forgive me."

"I understand perfectly. You saw how your guests behaved that evening at your party. They kept talking to themselves. They did not even realize how impolite that was. Mind you, I had told them that I'd be happy to be the interpreter. Oh well...."

IN THE LAND OF THE SWISS

"What do you think it is?" I asked. But before Anna could respond, the telephone rang. I looked at my watch. Whoops! It was almost eight o'clock. I had no idea I had been there so long.

"It's your husband, wondering if you've forgotten him completely," said Anna, handing the receiver to me. I told him that I was "on my way." Anna immediately took the receiver again and invited him over for a supper of soup and cake.

Again, Anna Buechli had taken over the situation and handled it with ease and spontaneity. The three of us had a simple and relaxed supper, parting for the evening as friends.

"So, what made you change your mind about her so fast?" asked my husband as we walked back to our apartment.

"She herself," I replied. "She is the exception in this culture—which proves the rule, I suppose. I really should not make up my mind about others anymore, until I get to know them." It felt good to confess. "The strangest thing is that it's a Swiss, of all people, who has to teach me how to be spontaneous! I certainly didn't expect that to happen."

— *1979* —

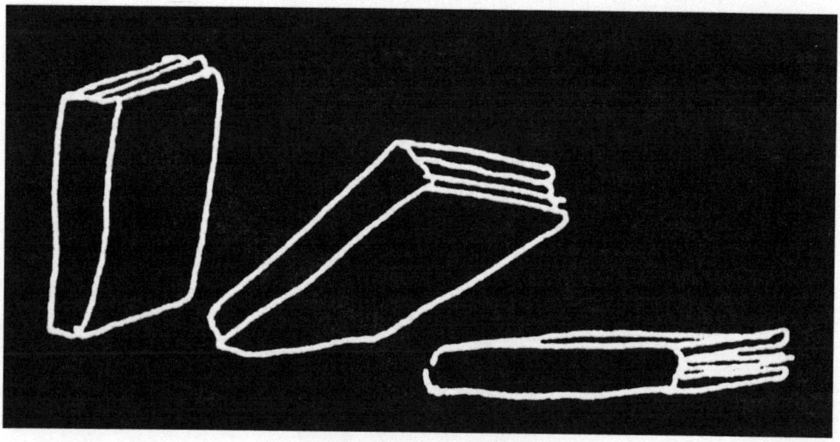

HERR PROFESSOR'S BIRTHDAY

Cars were parked on both sides of the narrow road that led up the hill to the restaurant. At the main entrance stood two liveried attendants, greeting everyone and directing them to the dining room. The restaurant had a magnificent view of the Lake of Zurich. It was here that Herr Professor Dr. Boddendorf's eightieth birthday celebration was to be held.

My husband and I were invited because the professor had taken an interest in my husband, who was a colleague. We had been invited a few times to his home. Each time it was to meet and honor a fellow scientist. Professor Boddendorf himself was said to be a scientist of extraordinary caliber. It was a surprise to his colleagues and friends that he had not yet been awarded a Nobel Prize.

The gatherings at his home were simple; white wine and hors d'oeuvres were served. Mrs Boddendorf, quite handsome in her seventies, moved about graciously, gently urging people to have one more stuffed mushroom or an open sandwich with smoked ham or shrimp. She had a slight stoop, which she carried elegantly. She always had a kind word or two for me, who obviously felt a bit out of place in the august company of her husband's guests.

Each time we met, Mrs Boddendorf told me the same little story about their visit to India, when her husband was invited to chair an international congress in nuclear physics. They were being driven to Agra to see the Taj Mahal when a family of monkeys had jumped down from a treetop onto the motor road and grimaced at them.

Professor Boddendorf talked to me directly only once. "Why is it," he asked me, "that the hot countries such as India use so many spices in their food?" But he was not listening when I explained the theory that spices help to preserve the food in hot climates. He rarely listened to anyone unless the conversation was about serious science, to which many of us had a hard time listening.

I had agreed to come to Professor Boddendorf's birthday celebration partly because I was curious about the food and the guests. The restaurant was well known for its cuisine and atmosphere. But mostly, I wanted to see what the wives of the European scientists were like. There had to be some, like myself, who were not part of the crowd. Perhaps I would be able to sit with one of them and together we could make our observations and form our opinions.

As we were ushered to the dining room, the rays of the setting sun were striking the expensive crystal on the tables near the windows overlooking the lake. The tables were exquisitely set with silver, embroidered linens, and fresh roses. The bouquet at each table was different. A smartly-dressed young woman stood at the door asking for our names and directing us to our assigned seats. My husband and I were separated by several tables. He was chosen to sit at the head table, where the professor himself would sit.

I found my name embossed on one of ten cards on a round table. A guest, a man of forty or so, was standing behind the chair to the right of mine. A couple, also about forty, stood opposite. We introduced ourselves and sat down. The man to my right helped me with my chair. His last name was that of the professor's.

"Are you, by any chance, related to Professor Boddendorf?" I asked.

"Yes, we are related," he replied. "I am his second son. My wife could not attend, so they put me outside the family table. But I am happy to be here." He seemed to be studying me. "You must be from India or Pakistan."

"India." I turned to greet the newest arrivals to the table, but I cast a glance back to my neighbor, the son of the great man.

Well-dressed waiters began to move around the room with bottles of white and red wine, filling our glasses. A trail of waitresses followed, serving salad. An elderly gentleman at the head table, where the guest of honor, his wife, and his closest friends were sitting, tapped his wine glass with a fork to attract our attention. The sound of conversation melted to a hum, and then to a whisper.

"Meine Damen und Herren..." He spoke at least ten minutes, welcoming us to this joyous and momentous occasion in celebration of the birthday of such a great man. He urged us to enjoy ourselves and thanked the professor, his wife, and the family for attending the celebration. Following the speech we all raised our glasses. The young Mr. Boddendorf then raised his to me.

"*Prost,*" he said, then paused. "Do you know my father?"

"Yes,—slightly. It's my husband who knows your father well. I got invited as his wife, I suppose." I had an urge to say more. "I've been to your parents' home a few times."

"You are lucky to be invited to my parents' home. Are you in physics?" he asked. "They usually don't mix with people who are not scientists."

"My husband is in nuclear medicine. My own field is very different from physics, actually. But tell me, what do you do?" Something about Mr. Boddendorf's manners made me bold enough to ask such a direct question. Before he could respond, the empty salad plates were removed and the soup was being served. I reconsidered, and chose a more neutral topic.

"Do you know if there will be a program afterwards?"

"I am sure. My father and his friends never miss a chance to lecture people. You must have noticed when you visited them."

His voice betrayed a bitterness that shocked me. I picked up the menu, pretending that I must learn all about the soup. The main ingredient was a wild, seasonal variety of mushroom that grows only on the slopes of the French Alps.

"*En Guete,*" I said, to the whole table, before taking my first spoonful.

"Oh, you speak Schweizer Deutsch[38]," said the woman across from me, and spoke a few words in that dialect.

"Not really. I can only say those two words. I can follow a bit, if I listen carefully."

Someone raised a glass. "*Prost.*" I turned to the man on my left, but he seemed engrossed in conversation with the woman on his left. So I turned again to my neighbor on the right and smiled.

"You asked me about my profession a minute ago, yes?" He had not forgotten. "I teach carpentry to middle school children,

---

[38] The German dialect of northern and northeastern Switzerland. It dates back to the middle ages.

something of which my father is very ashamed." It was uncomfortable for me to listen to these revealing statements about the father-son relationship. Fortunately, the next course arrived. We were served poached salmon with dill sauce and capers. The capers dotted one part of the plate and a sprig of fresh dill graced another. It was a work of art.

"How beautifully they serve here," I said, in genuine admiration.

"Oh yes," said Mr. Boddendorf, smiling. "This place is famous for its elegance. My father's disciples took great care. For his birthday, nothing is too good. *Prost.*" He raised his glass, looking a bit more relaxed.

"I gather you and your father are not in full agreement about things. Your fields are so different...."

"You have noticed. Yes, we are as far apart as a father and son could be. Do you know that when I refused to take physics as my major in college, he stopped talking to me for a whole month? He had tried the same thing with my older brother, who simply left home and went to France to study art. I dropped out and went to the Polytechnic to learn cabinet-making. I can understand his feelings. But now he prefers not to mention our names, let alone to introduce us to his friends." He picked up his glass and took a long sip of wine.

I tried to do justice to the beautiful salmon and concentrated on eating. The uneasiness in the air lingered. The man was determined to use this opportunity to pour out his problems to a stranger.

"It must be hard for you to attend this dinner, if your relationship with your father is so strained," I said in sympathy.

"Well, I didn't want to come. But my mother called and urged me to, because it would look bad if I didn't. So I agreed, on condition I didn't have to sit at the table with them. I'm here for her sake only." His expression changed. "You must have noticed how my mother walks. For many years now she has not been able to stand straight. She is so much under his pressure." A waiter came to clear the fish plates.

"Yes, I did wonder if she had some physical problem. But she carries it well. Your mother is a lovely woman. A woman of a generation in which wives felt fulfilled in their husbands' glory.

Of course, I know nothing about her background." I realized I had said too much. Perhaps I had touched a nerve.

"Did you know that my mother was once a concert pianist?" he asked. "My father heard her in a performance and he would not stop until she said yes to marriage. The man is determined, otherwise he couldn't rise this high. I hear he might get a Nobel Prize. Well, they better hurry. He won't live forever."

"So your mother left her career as a musician to marry your father?" The absence of choices for a woman of her time became sharp in my eyes. Did she really have no choice? "It's really sad," I said, "how women had to sacrifice their talents when choosing between love and work."

The meat course had just arrived. The plates were kept in quilted linens because they were very hot. Four little triangles of lamb chop, with small red potatoes sprinkled with fresh chives, and a group of tiny squash, made a composition that was pleasing and aromatic. I wished I hadn't eaten anything prior to this dish. Its invitation, reluctantly, I had to refuse. I nibbled a bit and watched how my neighbors, with great attention and pleasure, ate all of it.

"Don't worry if you cannot eat all this rich food," said Mr. Boddendorf, solicitously. "As usual, they overdid it. You need a Swiss stomach to eat and digest so much food."

"Oh, no, no. It's excellent food," I replied. "I just don't have an appetite big enough for a five-course meal." I signaled the waiter for some mineral water. "So, let's talk about your mother. I'm interested in women who marry brilliant men and leave their own careers behind. I wonder if they are content." Now it was I who had steered the discussion back to unpleasant subjects.

The waiters came with bottles of a different red wine—to accompany the lamb. I had begun to feel the effect of all the drinking and eating. So, when the man opposite me raised his glass, I merely sipped my mineral water.

"I wish you had known my mother twenty years ago," said my neighbor. "She didn't have a stoop then. She used to argue with Father over things, including our choice of studies. But the man never listened to her. We, my brother and I, watched how, slowly and gradually, she gave up having her own voice. She became nothing but his shadow. I wonder now if she has any sense of this change." His own voice was heavy.

There was more tapping of fork against wine glass to attract our attention. Everyone seemed glad to have a break from all the food, wine, and conversation. Chairs were pushed away from the tables slightly. This time it was Herr Professor himself who spoke. He toasted the guests and thanked his hosts, the friends who had organized this wonderful party for him. He made a few jokes about being eighty and the reduction of his brain cells. Then he sat down again.

I looked at Mrs Boddendorf on his left, sitting with a demure smile on her lips. It was impossible to determine how content she might really be. From this distance she looked perfectly happy. A grey-haired gentleman rose to give the next toast and speech. So it went for the next forty minutes.

The young Boddendorf moved in his chair impatiently. He looked at me as if to say, "Here they go again." I shrugged. I knew he wanted to talk more. We would still have time: the cheese and fruit, dessert, and coffee were still to come.

When the speeches ended, the waiters reappeared with trays of fruit and crackers and the choicest Swiss and French cheeses. I declined the plate, and turned again to Mr. Boddendorf.

"Tell me, do you ever have an opportunity to see your mother alone and have a personal talk?"

"Rarely," he said. "Last time she came to our house was six months ago, when my wife and I had our wedding anniversary. Father was away in Germany for some meeting. I went and picked her up and tried to talk a bit in the car. But she carefully changed the topic, asking me about *us.*" He cut into a piece of cheese with his knife, but did not eat it. "She makes me more upset than my father. At least he is what he is, but she is only a shell of what she used to be. Sometimes I feel like screaming in front of a crowd like this and telling them what a cruel and selfish man this genius is. Only we the family know." He left his grapes uneaten, too.

I now felt anxious for this long, drawn-out meal—and the son's confession—to end. I was uneasy about being influenced by this man's story about his father. All the time I had known the old man I had very little to do with him. I was able to ignore his glory and fame, but now suddenly I felt unable to ignore his vices.

IN THE LAND OF THE SWISS

As I mused, the last course, a sliver of raspberry torte, came and went, and the liqueurs and brandy were served. Men, many of them, were lighting their cigars and pipes. I was exhausted, and now began to develop a headache, which was aggravated when the tapping of the fork and glass occurred again.

This time, mercifully, the speeches were brief; most were notes of thanks. Someone at the head table got up and read a brief inscription from a parchment, telling of the professor's unparalleled contribution to science. The parchment was then presented to him.

The meal and the celebration came to an end at last. I shook hands with everyone at our table. Mr. Boddendorf held my hand a few seconds. "Thank you for listening to me," he said. "It was a great pleasure meeting you."

* * *

"Did you have a good time?" my husband asked in the car, going home.

"Oh—interesting," I said. "But it gave me a headache." I gazed out the window.

The rest of the drive was quiet.

— 1980 —

Epilogue

Two decades have passed since the last event in this book. The reckoning of my heart continues in my work as a Jungian psychotherapist and writer. The rigorous observations of fellow human beings and myself still reflect the anthropologist in me. The Khasis, the Bengalis, the Californians and the Swiss that I encountered are fond nostalgic memories that still deepen my responses to other cultures. Strangers no longer challenge me as strange; but the familiar sometimes become strange. I differentiate more easily the outer, the other, the inner, the familiar. Anthropology and Depth Psychology join to create new adventures of self-realization.

ABOUT THE AUTHOR

Manisha Roy, Ph.D. is a Bengali who was born in northeast Assam, India, and educated in Calcutta and the United States. Once an anthropologist, she is now a writer and lecturer in analytical psychology. She has been a practicing psychotherapist in the Boston area since 1985. She is the author of *Bengali Women* (Chicago, 1976, rev. 1992) and co-editor, with Lena Ross, of *Cast the First Stone: Ethics in Analytic Practice* (Chiron, 1995). She lives in Boston, Massachusetts, with her husband, Dr. Carl von Essen.